TREKKING THE
CAMÍ DELS BONS HOMES

GR107 – CROSSING THE PYRENEES
IN THE CATHARS' FOOTSTEPS

by Nike Werstroh and Jacint Mig

JUNIPER HOUSE, MURLEY MOSS,
OXENHOLME ROAD, KENDAL, CUMBRIA LA9 7RL
www.cicerone.co.uk

© Nike Werstroh and Jacint Mig 2024
First edition 2024
ISBN: 978 1 78631 223 5

Printed in China on responsibly sourced paper on behalf of Latitude Press Ltd
A catalogue record for this book is available from the British Library.
All photographs are by the authors unless otherwise stated.

Route mapping by Lovell Johns www.lovelljohns.com

The routes of the GR®, PR® and GRP® paths in this guide have been reproduced with the permission of the Fédération Française de la Randonnée, holder of the exclusive rights of the routes. The names GR®, PR® and GRP® are registered trademarks. © FFRP 2024 for all GR®, PR® and GRP® paths appearing in this work.

Contains OpenStreetMap.org data © OpenStreetMap contributors, CC-BY-SA. NASA relief data courtesy of ESRI

Updates to this guide

While every effort is made by our authors to ensure the accuracy of guidebooks as they go to print, changes can occur during the lifetime of an edition. Any updates that we know of for this guide will be on the Cicerone website (www.cicerone.co.uk/1223/updates), so please check before planning your trip. We also advise that you check information about such things as transport, accommodation and shops locally. Even rights of way can be altered over time.

The route maps in this guide are derived from publicly available data, databases and crowd-sourced data. As such they have not been through the detailed checking procedures that would generally be applied to a published map from an official mapping agency, although naturally we have reviewed them closely in the light of local knowledge as part of the preparation of this guide.

We are always grateful for information about any discrepancies between a guidebook and the facts on the ground, sent by email to updates@cicerone.co.uk or by post to Cicerone, Juniper House, Murley Moss, Oxenholme Road, Kendal LA9 7RL.

Register your book: To sign up to receive free updates, special offers and GPX files where available, create a Cicerone account and register your purchase via the 'My Account' tab at www.cicerone.co.uk.

Front cover: Montségur with its castle perched high on top of the mountain

CONTENTS

ROUTE SUMMARY TABLE

Stage	Start	Finish	Distance (km)	Ascent (m)	Descent (m)	Time	Page
1	Foix/ Montgaillard	Roquefixade	18	1040	700	5hr 30min	26
2	Roquefixade	Montségur	20	1020	860	6hr 30min	32
3	Montségur	Comus	16	1120	875	4hr 30min	38
4	Comus	Orlu	28	940	1270	8hr	42
5	Orlu	Mérens-les-Vals	17	1045	735	5hr	47
6	Mérens-les-Vals	Porta	25	1750	1385	9hr	53
7	Porta	Bellver de Cerdanya	36	1170	1660	10hr 30min	61
8	Bellver de Cerdanya	Bagà	24	1050	1195	7hr	68
9	Bagà	Gósol	24	1250	700	7hr	74
10	Gósol	Santuari de Queralt, Berga	29	1330	1605	9hr	81
Total			**237**	**11,715**	**10,985**	**72hr**	

Acknowledgements

We would like to thank Karina Behar from the Regulatory Council of Camí dels Bons Homes for the fantastic help and enthusiastic support during our research. Thank you to Caroline Bayard and Juliette Marcilloux from Ariège Tourisme for their great help and useful tips. Thank you for our hosts for the warm hospitality in France and in Catalonia.

Thank you to Joe Williams and everyone from the Cicerone team who believed in this project and worked on this book.

Mountain safety

Every mountain walk has its dangers, and those described in this guidebook are no exception. All who walk or climb in the mountains should recognise this and take responsibility for themselves and their companions along the way. The author and publisher have made every effort to ensure that the information contained in this guide was correct when it went to press, but, except for any liability that cannot be excluded by law, they cannot accept responsibility for any loss, injury or inconvenience sustained by any person using this book.

International distress signal *(emergency only)*
Six blasts on a whistle (and flashes with a torch after dark) spaced evenly for one minute, followed by a minute's pause. Repeat until an answer is received. The response is three signals per minute followed by a minute's pause.

Helicopter rescue
The following signals are used to communicate with a helicopter:

 Help needed:
raise both arms
above head to
form a 'Y'

 Help not needed:
raise one arm
above head, extend
other arm downward

Emergency telephone numbers
If telephoning from the UK the dialing codes are:
France: 0033; *Spain:* 0034

France: Emergency services tel 112
Catalonia: Emergency services tel 112; Guardia Civil for mountain rescue services and other accidents tel 062

Weather reports
France: www.meteo.fr
Catalonia: www.meteo.cat; www.meteoblue.com

Mountain rescue can be very expensive – be adequately insured.

Overview profile/staging options

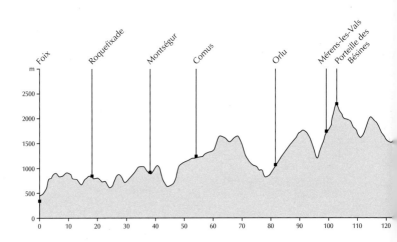

	Foix/Montgaillard to Roquefixade	Roquefixade to Montségur	Montségur to Comus	Comus to Orlu	Orlu to Mérens-les-Vals	Mérens-les-Vals to Porta
10 DAYS	*18km* *5hr 30min*	*20km* *6hr 30min*	*16km* *4hr 30min*	*28km* *8hr*	*17km* *5hr*	*25km* *9hr*

	Foix/Montgaillard to Roquefixade	Roquefixade to Montségur	Montségur to Comus	Comus to Orlu	Orlu to Mérens-les-Vals	Mérens-les-Vals to Porta
12 DAYS	*18km* *5hr 30min*	*20km* *6hr 30min*	*16km* *4hr 30min*	*28km* *8hr*	*17km* *5hr*	*25km* *9hr*

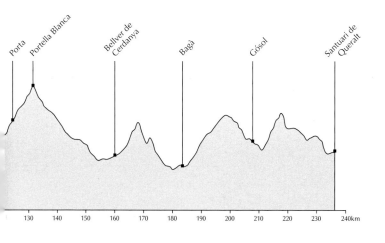

Porta to Bellver de Cerdanya	Bellver de Cerdanya to Bagà	Bagà to Gósol	Gósol to Santuari de Queralt, Berga
36km *10hr 30min*	*24km* *7hr*	*24km* *7hr*	*29km* *9hr*

AVERAGE DAY – 24km / 7hr 30min

Porta to Viliella	Viliella to Bellver de Cerdanya	Bellver de Cerdanya to Bagà	Bagà to Gósol	Gósol to Peguera	Peguera to Santuari de Queralt, Berga
22km *+ 2km to Viliella* *6hr 30min*	*14km* *3hr*	*24km* *6hr 30min*	*24km* *6hr 30min*	*18km* *5hr 30min*	*11km* *3hr 30min*

AVERAGE DAY – 20kmkm / 6hr

STAGE FACILITIES PLANNER

Stage	Place	Altitude (m)	Walking time	Cum. stage time
1	**Montgaillard**	**442**	**0hr**	**0hr**
1	Leychert	630	4hr 30min	4hr 30min
1	**Roquefixade**	**765**	**1hr**	**5hr 30min**
2	Montferrier	690	3hr 30min	3hr 30min
2	**Montségur**	**925**	**3hr**	**6hr 30min**
3	**Comus**	**1165**	**4hr 30min**	**4hr 30min**
4	Prades	1245	1hr	1hr
4	Montaillou	1280	30min	1hr 30min
4	Sorgeat	1050	4hr 30min	6hr
4	Ascou	1015	20min	6hr 20min
4	Orgeix	830	1hr	7hr 20min
4	**Orlu**	**835**	**40min**	**8hr**
5	**Mérens-les-Vals**	**1150**	**2hr**	**5hr**
6	Refuge des Bésines	2095	4hr	4hr
6	*L'Hospitalet prés-l'Andorre (1.5km off route)*	*1430*	*6hr 55min*	
6	*Porte-Puymorens (2km off route)*	*1600*	*4hr 40min*	
6	**Porta**	**1510**	**5hr**	**9hr**
7	Cabane de Campcardós	1950	1hr 30min	1hr 30min
7	*Viliella (2km from Molí del Salt)*	*1505*	*6hr*	
7	Prullans	1115	8hr	9hr 30min
7	**Bellver de Cerdanya**	**1010**	**1hr**	**10hr 30min**
8	Talló	1060	20min	20min
8	Refugi Cortals de l'Ingla	1600	2hr 30min	2hr 50min
8	Refugi Sant Jordi	1560	1hr	3hr 50min
8	**Bagà**	**785**	**3hr 10min**	**7hr**
9	Refugi Vents del Cadí	920	1hr	1hr
9	**Gósol**	**1430**	**6hr**	**7hr**
10	L'Espà	1325	1hr	1hr
10	*Peguera (about 5km off route)*	*1615*	*4hr 30min*	
10	**Santuari de Queralt**	**1125**	**8hr**	**9hr**
10	Berga	705	45min	9hr 45min

Legend: ○ hotel ▲ gîte/chambres d'hôtes/refuge △ campsite 🍴 refreshments 🛒 shop ▣ train station ◉ bus service 𝑖 information

Distance (km)	Cum. stage distance (km)	Facilities							
		Hotel	Gîte	Campsite	Refresh.	Shop	Train	Bus	Info
0	**0**	○		△	🍴	🛒	▣		
14	14	○							
4	**18**		▲		🍴				
11	11		▲		🍴	🛒			
9	**20**		▲	△	🍴	🛒			
9	**16**		▲	△	🍴				
4	4				🍴				
2	6		▲		🍴				
15.2	21.2		▲	△	🍴				
1.8	23		▲						
2.8	25.8				🍴				
2.2	**28**		▲	△	🍴				
5.5	**17**		▲	△	🍴	🛒	▣		
8.8	8.8		▲		🍴				
			▲	△	🍴	🛒	▣		
			▲		🍴		▣		
16	**25**	○	▲		🍴		▣		
4.5	4.5		▲						
			▲						
8.3	30.3	○		△	🍴	🛒			
5.7	**36**	○	▲		🍴	🛒		◉	𝑖
1.8	1.8	○			🍴				𝑖
8	9.8		▲		🍴				
3.8	13.6		▲		🍴				
10.4	**24**	○		△	🍴	🛒		◉	𝑖
4.5	4.5		▲		🍴				
19	**24**	○	▲	△	🍴	🛒		◉	𝑖
3.8	3.8	○						◉	
			▲						
11	**29**				🍴				
3	32	○			🍴	🛒		◉	𝑖

Easy to follow path leads the way towards the Bésines valley and mountain hut (Stage 6)

INTRODUCTION

The narrow path heading towards sheer cliffs below the peak of Gallina Pelada (Stage 10)

The majestic Pyrenees, forming a natural border between France and Spain, have lots to offer for outdoor lovers all year round. Blanketed in snow in the winter, the many ski slopes come to life. And when the white blanket melts away, fresh mountain streams race down the slopes, wildflowers carpet the meadows and hikers replace the skiers. Summer is the perfect time to explore this wild frontier that treats hikers to myriad trails and breathtaking panorama.

Long-distance trails traverse the entire length of the mountain range but there are some equally beautiful shorter trails that cross the mountains. Not surprisingly, many of the steep narrow trails were used from the medieval times and up to the Spanish Civil War or during World War 2 as escape routes.

Starting in southern France, the GR107, Camí dels Bons Homes or Chemin des Bonshommes (Way of the Good Men), visits fascinating castle ruins perched on rocks and then takes you through tranquil hamlets before it weaves its way across the Pyrenees to the Catalan town of Berga.

The trail was created with the intention of connecting towns and villages with a Cathar history. The religious group had a significant number of followers in southern France, especially in the Languedoc area (the modern-day region of Occitanie) during the 12–14th centuries. Before long, the Catholic Church felt threatened by the movement which was not just attracting the poor but also had many noble supporters. In 1209 the Pope declared a crusade against the heretics (see the brief history of the Cathars below). Thousands were killed, and after the siege of Montségur (1244), many of the remaining Cathars fled France and crossed the Pyrenees to seek refuge in Spain. They settled in great numbers in the Catalan towns of Bagà, Gósol and Berga.

Arguably the Cathars could have taken numerous routes across the Pyrenees. However, it is fascinating to believe that some might have walked these paths all those centuries ago.

As well as the interesting history, people have always been captivated by the varied landscape.

The remarkable GR107 was voted as the third best GR route in France in 2022 in the competition 'Mon GR Préféré'. Each year people can choose the best 'Grande Randonnée' from 10 carefully selected trails.

The GR107 trail can be walked in both directions, and you will find that while the French mostly walk the trail from Foix, the Catalans will start the trail in Berga. Therefore French websites describe the trail from Foix, and Catalan websites suggest that the trail starts from Berga. However, as the trail is based on Cathar history and the Cathars fled from France, it felt right that we started the trek from Foix.

During less troubled times, the trail was used to connect people living and working in the tiny hamlets and villages. Modern-day hikers are fortunate enough to be able to enjoy the beauty of the landscape without fearing for their lives.

As you cross this unforgettable landscape you will no doubt enjoy some friendly hospitality, sample some tasty local food, talk to fellow hikers and admire the magnificent scenery on both sides of the Pyrenees.

A BRIEF HISTORY OF THE CATHARS

The word 'Cathars' derives from the Ancient Greek word *kathari* and means the 'pure ones'. The Cathars were also known as Albigensians. This name comes from the town of Albi which was one of the Cathar centres.

The roots of Catharism can be traced back to Manichaeism, which originated from the Middle East and reached Europe via the Silk Road. These beliefs were incorporated with Christian beliefs, and Catharism had many followers in southern Europe by the 12th century.

The Cathars – who referred to themselves as Good Christians – were dualists. They believed that the good God created everything immaterial and that the evil God was responsible for everything material and perishable. They rejected wealth and led an ordinary simple life. Most of them were vegetarians but some ate

fish. They didn't have church buildings and the spiritual leaders – the Perfecti Parfaits (men) and Parfaites (women) selected from the believers – guided other ordinary members to achieve the rewards of belief and practice. The Perfecti (*bonhommes*/ good men) led a very ascetic life, and worked as manual traders. Celibacy was practised by the Perfecti; as the Cathars believed in reincarnation, they thought that the soul would be repeatedly reborn until it rejected the material world. They believed that a man could be reborn as a woman and vice versa. The immaterial and sexless spirit was important to the Cathars. They believed women were equally capable of being spiritual leaders.

By the 12th century the Cathar religion had taken root and was gaining more and more adherents in the Languedoc, known at the time for its high culture, tolerance and liberalism. Tolerated – and even supported – by a number of nobles in the Languedoc area, the growing number of Cathars became a real threat to the Catholic Church. From 1147, papal legates were sent to the area to try (unsuccessfully) to win people back to the Catholic Church.

Pope Innocent III (1161–1216) urged Raymond VI (1156–1222), the count of Toulouse, to act against the heresy. A papal legate, Pierre de Castelnau, who was sent to deal with Raymond's tolerance for the Cathars, was murdered in 1208. Raymond was thought to be responsible so he was excommunicated, and Pope Innocent called for a crusade against

13

the heretics. The army, led by nobles of the north – who were promised the lands of the south after the Cathars were gone – began their persecution. The first significant massacre took place in 1209, in and around Béziers where some twenty thousand were killed and the town was burnt down. During the crusade, whole towns were often burnt down, killing both Cathar and Catholic inhabitants.

The Treaty of Paris (1229) officially ended the crusade. The Counts of Toulouse were dispossessed. However, despite 20 years of persecution, the Cathars were not completely erased from the region, and in 1233 an inquisition was established to hunt down the remaining followers.

The fortress of Montségur was one of the centres of the Cathars. Perched high on rocks, it housed some five hundred people, including more than two hundred Perfectis. In May 1243 the fortress was besieged for nine months, and in March 1244 the Perfectis were all burnt at the foot of the castle.

The remaining Cathar communities continued to live in more secrecy during the 13th and 14th centuries, but many fled to Italy and Spain where conditions were less cruel.

To learn more about the Cathars visit:

www.cathar.info
www.worldhistory.org/Cathars/

or read *The Perfect Heresy: The Life and Death of the Cathars* by Stephen O'Shea.

Following the path between Orlu and Mérens-les-Vals (Stage 5)

THE GR107 TRAIL

The trail starts from Foix in southern France, crossing over the Pyrenees and then through the Serra de Moixeró to the town of Berga in Catalonia. The first part of the 237km trail visits some castle ruins and meanders through fields and hamlets, but before long you are climbing the slopes of Pyrenees.

One of the highest mountain ranges in Europe, the Pyrenees were formed by the collision between the European Plate and the Iberian microplate during the Paleogene period (some 55 to 25 million years ago). After the uplift, intense erosion and isostatic readjustments shaped the chain.

The highest point of the trail is at Portella Blanca (2517m), where the three countries of France, Andorra and Spain meet. You then walk through the lower Serra de Moixeró range, formed during the late Paleozoic continental collision. And then, on the tracks between Bagà and Gósol, you have plenty of time to admire Pedraforca, an emblematic mountain that is somehow separated from the Pre-Pyrenees.

The long-distance GR107 route was created in 1998, with the intention of connecting towns and villages with Cathar history. The trail is managed by the Regulatory Council of Camí dels Bons Homes, an autonomous organization that also helps to promote the route and the network of services that cater for hikers along the trail. The Regulatory Council works together with Pyrénées Ariège Tourisme in France.

This is a great trek for anyone who want to do a multi-day hike through the majestic Pyrenees without the need to carry a tent, as the trail is divided into 10 stages (or 10 days), and each stage finishes in a village or town where accommodation can be found. There are some long days (Stage 7, Porta to Bellver de Cerdanya, and Stage 10, Gósol to Berga) which can be divided up if you would prefer shorter days. Options for shortening these stages are mentioned in the book, and the 12 day itinerary gives you a more comfortable pace with more time to explore the historical towns.

A short taxi ride can also help to cut down the kilometres at some stages (for example Stages 7, 8 and 10). Make sure you book your pick-up: www.taxitrail.com.

It is also possible to tackle only half of the trail – for example, between Foix and Porta, or between Berga and Bellver de Cerdanya, as there are train or bus services to and from these towns. Some sections of the trail are long and demanding, so a reasonable level of fitness is required for the trek.

PLANTS AND FLOWERS

Red pine, fir and beech can be found on the lower slopes of the Pre-Pyrenees in the Cadí-Moixeró Natural Park. Above 1800m, black pine is the most common species, and alpine meadows usually replace trees above 2000m.

In the summer, spectacular alpine flowers bloom on the slopes

*Clockwise from top left: Cornflower (*Centaurea montana*), Early purple orchid (*Orchis mascula*), Bee orchid (*Ophrys apifera*), Dusky crane's bill (*Geranium phaeum*), Spotted orchid (*Dactylorhiza maculata*), Burnt-tip orchid (*Neotinea ustulata*), Chamomile (*Chamaemelum nobile*)*

of the Pyrenees. From late May you can spot delicate orchids, such as the bee orchid and the early spider orchid, among many others. You may also find several varieties of gentians flowering throughout the season. The limestone provides a perfect home for many alpine plants, such as species of the saxifrage and thistles, and on the meadows you can admire different species of lilies.

Pink rhododendrons and yellow gentians are common in the Ariège Pyrenees. In Gorges de la Frau (Stage 3), you might spot the yellow flowers of the endemic Galle poppy.

The Pyrenees Ramondia only grows in the Pyrenees and is often found on the shaded slopes between 1000 and 1800m. It is also known as 'bears' ears' because of its rounded leaves.

The tough Pyrenean mountain pines can push the treeline up to 2600m in the Pyrenees. Black pines can be found up to 2100m, and on lower slopes Scots pine, beech and birch are the most common species.

WILDLIFE

When crossing the Pyrenees on the GR107 in the late spring or summer, you can almost certainly spot two iconic mammals: the shy Pyrenean chamois, skilfully navigating the steep slopes, and the alpine marmots. The marmots were reintroduced to the Pyrenees in 1948, and they prefer the higher slopes between 1000m and 3200m. You will probably spot some as you are descending from Portella Blanca (Stage 7). Even if you don't see them, you might hear the whistling noises they make to communicate with each other. They spend the summer months eating to build up fat for the winter when they hibernate in their burrows for about seven months.

After bear numbers fell to only a handful in the 1990s, three brown bears from Slovenia were introduced to the Pyrenees. It is estimated that there are about 70 brown bears, mainly living in the central part of the Pyrenees. Their numbers are slowly growing.

There are a small number of grey wolves in the Pyrenees. Some live on the eastern part of the mountain range.

You can spot birds of prey such as the griffon vulture, which has an impressive two-and-a-half-metre wingspan, the bearded vulture and the golden eagle in the Ariège Pyrenees.

Snakes are usually wary of humans and many of them are harmless; however, there are some venomous snakes – such as the *Vipera seoanei*, or the asp viper– in the mountainous areas of northern Catalunya.

Cows, although not a wild animal, are often seen on the meadows where they graze during the warmer months. Never walk between calf and mother, and always give them a wide berth – at least 30 metres. Divert from the path if it is necessary and the terrain allows.

TRAVELLING TO AND FROM THE TRAIL

The closest airport is Toulouse in France. There are numerous flights to Toulouse from the UK, mainly from London airports but EasyJet also fly from Bristol. There are also flights from many European cities. You can fly to Barcelona from London, Birmingham and Manchester airports. Alternatively, fly to Carcassone or Bordeaux and take the train to Foix.

You can also take the Eurostar to Paris and then continue on the high speed TGV rail service to Toulouse. As always, shop around for the best deals. From Toulouse there is a regular train service to Foix (approximately a 1hr journey): www.sncf.com.

From Toulose airport you can get to the train station by a shuttle bus (approximately €9), or a cheaper option is to use public transport. A single ticket (€1.80) allows you to use trams and buses for 90 minutes. The T2 tram line that connects the airport with the city will reopen in 2026. Until then the numbers 30 and 31 buses will take you to the T1 tram line that goes towards Arenas. From here you can get Metro A to Matabiau train station (Marengo metro stop). Plan your route on www.tisseo.fr.

At the end of your trek in Berga, you can take a bus to Barcelona (journey time is approximately 2hr). Barcelona is well connected with other European cities and numerous airlines, including the well-known budget airlines, offer flights to and from various UK airports, including London, Birmingham and Manchester. Alternatively, Girona airport also offers flights to and from various UK airports such as London, Bristol, Bournemouth or East Midlands. If you need to get back to Toulouse, there is a bus service twice daily to Puigcerda. From Puigcerda take the train to the nearby Latour-de-Carol-Enveitg, and you can get the train to Toulouse from here (journey time 2hr 30min–3hr).

WHEN TO GO AND WHAT TO TAKE

As this trail crosses the Pyrenees which are blanketed in snow in the winter, the best time to walk the entire trail is between May and October. You might still find some snow patches on higher ground in late May. The busiest time on the trail is in July and August, so booking accommodation during these months is highly recommended. Some accommodation might close for the winter, while others will stay open as they cater for skiers.

It is essential to keep your bag as light as possible. However, as the trail crosses the Pyrenees, be prepared to experience variable weather. Take a fleece and waterproof jacket/poncho as part of your hiking gear as the evenings can be cool, even in the summer months. You will benefit from taking lightweight hiking clothes that you can rinse in the evening. The French side of the Pyrenees is known to be wetter and you will probably experience some rain that might come as an afternoon shower during the first half of the trek. A rain poncho can be very practical on this trail in summer. It is lightweight and you can quickly and easily cover yourself and your backpack. Your hiking boots/shoes will be the most important piece of gear, so make sure they are comfortable and reliable. You might want to take a pair of hiking sandals or flip flops for the evenings to give your feet a break from your boots.

Take a sleeping bag liner, as even if you are planning to stay at auberges and hotels there might be a stage where you will have to spend a night in a gîte or refuge where bedding might not be provided. You might prefer to take a sleeping bag if staying in refuges or dormitories every night. A small travel towel is also advisable as

they are usually not provided. A sun hat and sun cream are essential, and make sure you carry ample water for the day. This is especially important on the drier, warmer Spanish side of the trek.

If camping, you will need lightweight camping equipment: a tent, a sleeping bag, a sleeping mat and the essentials for cooking.

Download a route card from www.camidelsbonshomes.com and collect nine stamps at accommodations along the trail to receive a certificate of completion. There are also some discounts available for those collecting stamps. Check the website for details.

In case of emergency call 112. If you see a rescue helicopter and you don't need help, raise one arm above your head and extend the other arm

Approaching an unmanned shelter in the Campcardós valley, a popular rest stop, before continuing to Portella Blanca (Stage 7)

downward, forming a letter 'N'. If you or someone else nearby needs help, raise both arms above your head to form a letter 'Y'.

ACCOMMODATION AND FOOD

In France you are most likely to spend the night in a gîte, an auberge or a family-run chambre d'hotes. You will have limited choice on some sections – especially on the more remote French side of the trail – where there might only be one or two places to spend the night. Gîtes usually provide dormitory-style accommodation. However, some offer double rooms as well. Many of the family-run places offer a combination of different types of accommodation. Once you have crossed into Catalonia you will pass through towns with more choices.

It is best to book your accommodation in advance, especially during the summer months. There are some towns and villages where the suggested stage ends have limited choices. The first three stages of the trail, between Foix and Comus, are also shared with another long-distance trail with significant Cathar history, the Cathar Way (GR367). Therefore, pre-booking accommodation on these stages is highly recommended.

If you are willing to carry a tent there are some campsites and also some manned and unmanned refuges along the trail.

In France the trail goes through some small villages where you won't find cafés, restaurants or even shops, making it very difficult to get your own food. The good news is that all the accommodation listed in this

The Refuge des Bésines is a modern-looking manned hut on the Mérens–Porta section (Stage 6)

Looking back at the rugged mountain peaks towering above the Nabre river valley from L'Estagnas (Stage 6)

book caters for walkers. It is best to opt for half board, and there is also the option to buy a picnic lunch from your host. The evening meal is shared with fellow walkers, and is cooked and served by your host. Many of the hosts source the ingredients from local farmers and use seasonal fresh vegetables for the home-cooked meal. If you want to get a packed lunch, let your host know (the earlier the better, but at the latest when you arrive). As it is very difficult to get supplies on the French section of the trail, it is highly recommended that you buy all the food you need from your hosts. There might be drinking fountains in the villages but you cannot rely on them, so it is best to carry plenty of water.

Once you cross into Catalonia you can still opt for half board, but it is possible to buy food for the day as there are shops (and also cafés and restaurants) in Bellver de Cerdanya, Bagà, Gósol and in Berga.

A full list of accommodation along the trail is available at www.camidelsbonshomes.com in addition to the accommodation list in Appendix B.

LUGGAGE TRANSFER

Tour operators – if you book the trek with them – might provide luggage transfer.

However, there is no luggage transfer service available for the entire trail if you organize your own trip. For some sections, such as between Montségur and Comus and Orlu, some of the hosts can provide a luggage transfer. However, it can take an hour to cover a few kilometres between the settlements on the remote mountain roads, so this service can be pricey.

In Catalonia, Taxi Trail (www.taxi-trail.com, +34 686349857) offer help with luggage transfers. They also provide taxi services on the Spanish side of the trail, even to and from rural areas.

HIKING WITH A HORSE OR DONKEY

You can hire a donkey to accompany you on the trek, or you can ride a horse. For some sections of the GR107 trail you have to take the variant that is suitable for horse riding. These variants are marked at the junctions. There are several companies that organize horse treks along the trail.

If you want to hire a horse, check out www.soularac.com/produit/decouverte-pyrenees-cathares-cheval. If you want to hire a donkey, check these websites for more details: www.la-ferme-aux-anes.com/index.php or https://escapanes.com/randonnees/.

LANGUAGE

On this trail you will encounter three languages: French, Catalan and Spanish. In some villages in rural France some people might only speak French, but English will still be spoken, especially by younger people. Locals welcome tourists and you can get by with a few French words combined with English and some 'sign' language. In Catalonia most local people are bilingual and speak Catalan as well as Spanish. If you speak some basic Spanish you will have no problems in the rural areas. English is, however, widely spoken, especially among younger people.

Appendix C is a glossary of some basic French, Catalan and Spanish words that you might find useful.

MAPS AND WAYMARKING

The GR107 long-distance trail is well waymarked with red and white stripes. A red and white cross marks the wrong way at junctions and turnoffs. At junctions where there are other GR trails crossing the GR107, look out for the GR107 signs. Other local trails in the area are marked with different colours. The variants of the GR107 are usually marked at junctions, and in this guide we mention such variants.

As the trail is well signposted, the maps in this guide will probably suffice. You can also pick up a leaflet with a map in Foix before you start your trek. You can also buy an Editorial Alpina map for the trail: www.editorialalpina.com.

Some applications on your smartphone are worth considering such as Maps.me, Ign and Ign Rando.

USING THIS GUIDE

From Foix (France) to Berga (Catalonia), the trail is divided into 10 recommended stages. Information

The entire length of the route is characterized by good waymarking

boxes at the start of each stage provide the following information: start and finish point, distance, total ascent and descent, the length of the time the stage is likely to take, and details about refreshments and facilities. Shops and snack bars are mentioned if there are any in a village the trail passes through, but bear in mind that there aren't many on the French side and they might be closed when you are passing through. Always carry enough food for the day. You can also refer to the Stage Facilities Planner which summarises all the facilities and information for each stage.

The times provided – both for the stages themselves and between intermediary landmarks – are approximate and do not take account of longer breaks for picnics. As you are walking with a heavier backpack you might

23

need longer time to cover certain distances than if you were to go on a day walk. For some stages you might also need more frequent rest stops so always allow yourself plenty of daytime hours to complete the planned stage. Once you have started the trek using this guide, you will see how your own pace compared to the times given and can adjust your planning accordingly. Accommodation options are given in the facilities box, but in some places there might be some other options to choose from and it is highly recommended that you do some research before booking.

Appendices

Appendix A offers some useful contacts and information. Appendix B provides accommodation options along the route and a Catalan–Spanish–French–English glossary can be found in Appendix C.

GPX tracks

GPX tracks for the routes in this guidebook are available to download free at: www.cicerone.co.uk/1223/GPX. If you have not bought the book through the Cicerone website, or if you've bought the book without opening an account, please register your purchase in your Cicerone library to access GPX and update information.

A GPS device is an excellent aid to navigation, but you should also carry a map and a compass and know how to use them. GPX files are provided in good faith, but in view of the profusion of formats and devices, neither the author nor the publisher accepts responsibility for their use. We provide files in a single standard GPX format that works on most devices and systems, but you may need to convert files to your preferred format using a GPX converter, such as: www.gpsvisualizer. com or one of the many other apps and online converters available.

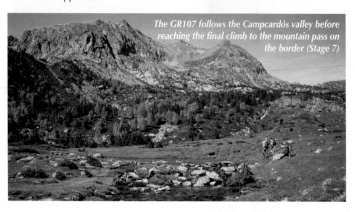

The GR107 follows the Campcardós valley before reaching the final climb to the mountain pass on the border (Stage 7)

THE GR107

Crossing the border into Catalonia through Portella Blanca at 2517m, the highest point on the trail (Stage 7)

STAGE 1
Foix/Montgaillard to Roquefixade

Start	Foix/Montgaillard
Finish	Roquefixade
Time	5hr 30min (plus allow another hour if you walk from Foix. Allow an extra 45min–1hr to visit the castle ruins above Roquefixade.)
Distance	18km (+4km from Foix)
Total ascent	1040m
Total descent	700m

Before you embark on your trek make sure to spend a day or two in Foix to explore the narrow streets of the old town and the imposing castle perched on the hilltop. The GR107 trail was originally marked from Foix but it went through private land and the first few kilometres are no longer available for public use. The trail has therefore been altered and now only starts in Montgaillard, some 4km from Foix. This first section of the trail eases you gently into the walking as you walk alongside fields and then through forest, with some gentle ascents and plenty of splendid views. Allow some time to climb to the ruins of Roquefixade castle where your efforts will be rewarded with far-reaching views.

FOIX CASTLE

Strategically built on the rocky hilltop in the late 10th century, the fortified castle overlooking Foix played a key role in medieval military history.

In 1002 Roger I, the count of Carcassonne, bequeathed the fortress to his son Bernard, and the castle became the count's residence until 1290. The castle helped to control the access to the upper Ariège valley and from 1034 it was the capital of the county of Foix. Many of the counts of Foix were known for supporting the Occitan resistance to the crusade against the Albigensians (Cathars), and Foix provided refuge to the Cathars between the 12th and 14th centuries.

Facilities Stage 1

	☼ ⛺ 🍴 🚉 ■ ■ ⓘ	Foix
	☼ ⛺ 🍴 🚉 ■	Montgaillard
4hr 30min	☼	Leychert
5hr 30min	⬆ 🍴	Roquefixade — Gîte d'Etape de Roquefixade (offers half board and packed lunch)

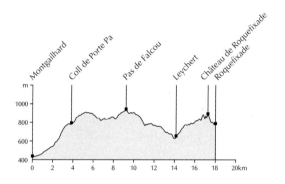

In the 12th and 13th centuries the castle only had the two square towers. The round tower was built in the 15th century. The interactive museum in the castle gives an insight into the castle's history and its counts, and its role in Cathar history. There are also several demonstrations of different aspects of the old life throughout the day. It is easy to spend all day there. However, it is possible to nip out for lunch and then return to the castle in the afternoon.

For more information, opening times and tickets check: www.sites-touristiques-ariege.fr/en/chateau-de-foix or www.ariegepyrenees.com.

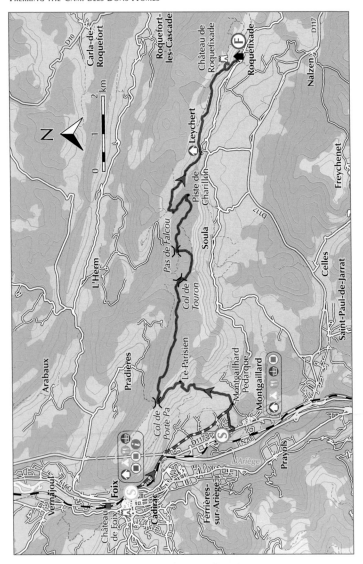

From Foix you can take a bus (Line 5) or taxi to Montgaillard. (Seek information in the Foix-Ariège-Pyrénées Tourist Office, 29 rue Téophile Delcassé 09000 Foix.)

There is a bus stop near the Forges de Pyrène (www.forges-de-pyrene.com) located along the D117 road. From the D117 take Chemin de Caussou and then keep right on Chemin du Stade and after passing a football pitch, reach D9A (Rte de Soula), where you keep right. You can walk from Foix if you follow the D117 road and then the D9A (Avenue de Roquafixade) from the roundabout. From Foix it is approximately 4km to the Montgaillard Pedarque junction.

Walk along the D9A road to **Montgaillard Pedarque** (457m, **1hr from Foix or 15min from Montgaillard**) junction with a picnic table beneath a tree and go left. From there you can easily follow the red and white GR signs. This part of the trail is shared with the GR367 (Sentier Cathar). Pass a house/barn and continue straight on with a stream on the left of the path. Keep left by the Piqeonnier signpost. Follow the GR signs, initially alongside pastures and then ascend among trees and bushes.

Turn right, up and away from the stream, and walk through forest, ignoring any unmarked path or path marked with 'X'. Climb the mountainside which is scattered with boulders slightly above you.

After a short climb enjoy the first amazing views towards the nearby mountains and all the way to Foix. Shortly after pass an overgrown ruin. About an hour from Montgaillard Pedarque junction reach a wide path at **Le Parisien** (758m, **1hr 15min**) and go left, signed towards Roquefixade (14km). Follow the broad track

Unobstructed views towards Montgaillard in the valley

for about 15min, with some views to Montgaillard in the valley with forest-covered mountains in the background, to reach **Col de Porte Pa** (797m, **1hr 30min**) and go right on the wide path. (There is a gate on the left to private land that the route used to go through. You might therefore see some old signs, but that route is no longer available to the public.)

About 20min later at the track junction go left and descend the forest track for about 30min, ignoring any other tracks marked with an 'X'. In the late spring and early summer look out for orchids. At the forest track junction continue straight on passing a brown sign, 'Route Forestière du Cap de Touron', and shortly after pass a forestry building. At **Col de Touron** junction (851m, **2hr 30min**) go right on the track signed towards Roquefixade.

Shortly after, leave the track to the left on the narrow grassy path. Walk across a field and then through forest and at Clot Des Bucs (840m) path junction continue straight on downhill. Keep left at Le Pech du Soula (890m) path junction and follow the marked forest path for about 10min to reach a track at **Pas de Falcou** (925m, **3hr**) and go right.

At the next junction keep right and a few minutes later at La Frontiere (910m), continue straight on downhill ignoring any other paths marked with an 'X'.

Arrive on a track at **Piste de Charillon** (770m) and go left. When the track splits take the right branch and at a junction near a house keep left. Pass a farm building and keep sharply right near a barn. Follow the GR signs at each track junction and less than an hour from Piste de Charillon, reach a tarmac road by a postbox in **Leychert** (**4hr 30min**).

The path goes under a sheer rock face before arriving in Roquefixade

Keep left and walk among houses for a few minutes and then go left by a shrine. Ascend away from the hamlet and follow the red and white signs to the right. As you follow the narrow path on the mountainside you can make out the castle of Roquefixade, and you can even spot Montségur castle perched on rocks in the distance. About 40min from the shrine in Leychert arrive on a wider path and go right and follow the GR signs to La Calme (848m) track junction, where you go right. Shortly after look out for a path with some steps on the left. It is marked as 'Route 1, 4' and you can take that to the ruins of **Château**

The ruins of Château de Roquefixade

de Roquefixade. Climbing to the ruins is highly recommended. Follow the steep narrow path to meet another path by the rocks, where you keep right towards the ruins. From the castle you can enjoy an extensive panorama.

CHÂTEAU DE ROQUEFIXADE

Records show that there might have been a **castle** on the cliffs from 1180, but the present ruins are more recent. This 'Cathar Castle', built on the cliff overlooking Roquefixade, might have provided shelter for the Cathars. However, the ruins you see today are later than this.

The castle was part of the line of royal fortresses built along the Corbières hills to guard the territory of the Count of Foix during the 13th century. The fortress was remodelled in the 14th century, with further alterations made in the 15th and 16th centuries. In 1632 the French king Louis XIII ordered the destruction of the castle as it was too costly to run and no longer served a purpose.

Allow at least 45min–1hr for the detour to the castle ruins. From the ruins retrace your steps to the track marked with GR signs and descend towards the village. Pass a viewpoint and then keep left by the cross towards Gîte d'Etape de Roquefixade. This is likely to be your accommodation for the night.

31

STAGE 2
Roquefixade to Montségur

Start	Roquefixade
Finish	Montségur
Time	6hr 30min, plus 1hr 30min to detour to Montségur castle
Distance	20km
Total ascent	1020m
Total descent	860m

Soon after you leave Roquefixade the castle ruins, perched on rocks above Montségur, come teasingly into view. This stage will take you through small quiet hamlets and lush forests with trickling streams. In dry weather it should be an easy stage, but save some energy to climb the steep hillside to the ruins of Château de Montségur just before arriving at the village.

Follow the GR signs among houses, leaving Roquefixade on the track. Shortly after pass a **World War 2 memorial** and then walk alongside pastures. The memorial commemorates the 16 young fighters for the resistance who died in July 1944 when their patrol was surprised by Germans.

About 30min from Roquefixade, reach the hamlet of **Coulzonne (30min)** and follow the surfaced road among houses, passing the old wash house. Before long you can make out Montségur castle perched on rocks in the distance as you descend on the country lane.

Meet and cross another tarmac road and continue on the forest track by the wooden sign, 'Foret de Mondini – Sentier Cathare'. Go through a gate and when the forest track splits, take the right branch uphill. Gradually the track narrows to a forest path.

This part of the path can get very muddy in the spring or after heavy rain. Keep right at the path junction, and less than an hour after you joined the forest path drop down to the D117 road just outside the hamlet of Conte (Nalzen). Cross the road and go left along the road. After 150m leave the D117 road to the right, cross

Facilities Stage 2

| 3hr 30min | ⬆ 🍴 ⊕ | Montferrier | Le Presbytère de Montferrier (gîte) |
| 6hr 30min | ⬆ ⛺ 🍴 ⊕ | Montségur | La Maison sous le Château (half board and packed lunch) |

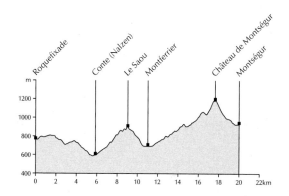

Gîte in Roquefixade, the only accommodation in the village

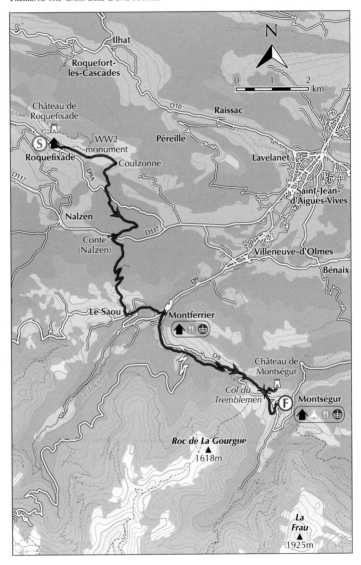

The trail on this stage can get really muddy after heavy rain

a bridge over a stream, and then keep left on a track signed towards Montségur. (50m to the right there is a restaurant, Les Sapins, where you might be able to get refreshments, although this is most likely to be closed at time of passing.)

Ignoring a path marked with an 'X', pass a house and follow the forest path, crossing a stream a few times on rocks before the path bends away from the stream. After a gentle ascent walk alongside fields and emerge onto a track through a gate and keep left. Once again you have views towards Montségur castle. About 1hr 15min after leaving the D117, arrive at a group of houses (**Le Saou**, **3hr 10min**) where the track becomes a tarmac lane. Follow the GR signs among houses. At the junction go left alongside a fence and about 80m later leave this tarmac lane on a path to the left. Shortly after, reach and cross the lane again and continue on the path on its other side. Meet and cross the tarmac lane several times and then descend near the stream.

About 20min from Le Saou, reach the tarmac road at the edge of **Montferrier** (**3hr 30min**). Keep right downhill along the road. Follow the GR signs through Montferrier. At the tarmac road junction keep left, and shortly after go right and over the bridge. After crossing the Le Touyre river turn sharply right, passing the entrance of a campsite. Notice the remains of the hydraulic forges below the bridge. Pass a parking area for campers and at Labarouse (714m) junction continue on a track straight on. Pass further houses, and at the junction continue straight on the narrow tarmac lane, ignoring other tracks.

35

Breathtaking views in the direction of Roquefixade

Descend with a pasture on the right. There are some houses on the other side of the stream on the left. There are some beehives near the path. At L'Escloupet (796m) path junction, take the path on the left signed for Montségur. Cross the stream twice on wooden bridges. Reach and cross a tarmac road and continue on its other side, straight on alongside the stream. There are a couple of wooden 'bridges' to assist you through this occasionally muddy section. Cross the stream several times on rocks and on wooden footbridges. At the path junction go sharply left. Shortly after a field on the right pass some houses. About 40min from L'Escloupet emerge onto the D9 tarmac road and keep right. The castle appears in front of you, perched on rock. Follow the snaking road for 10–15min and go left on a forest path marked with a GR sign. At **Col du Tremblemen** junction (1035m, **5hr 45min**) – before you continue on the GR107 – keep left and climb to **Château de Montségur**. (Allow at least 1hr to return to this junction.)

From the castle return to Col du Tremblemen junction and keep left to re-join the GR107 trail. Reach a tarmac road. Go left then keep right on a surfaced road and descend towards the village, passing the Cross of Ferrocas (named after a 19th-century blacksmith). Reach a tarmac road in **Montségur**. Turn right and follow the signs through the village, passing the wash house and a small archaeology museum.

CASTLE OF MONTSÉGUR (CHÂTEAU DE MONTSÉGUR)

The castle was in ruins for over 40 years before Raymond de Péreille, one of the lords of Montségur, decided to rebuild the fortification around 1204. The refortified castle then became a home to Guilhabert de Castres, a Cathar bishop, and by 1233 it was 'the seat and head' (*domicilium et caput*), a centre of Cathar activity. In 1242 a group of men from Montségur murdered two representatives of the inquisition, triggering military action. Troops were sent to the castle. The strategy was to besiege the castle, with the assumption that water and supplies would run out. However, the defenders were supported by the local population and the siege lasted for nine months. Eventually, after several attacks, the castle surrendered in March 1244. Some 220 Cathars – who refused to denounce the Cathar faith – were burnt at the foot of the mountain and the castle was destroyed. The ruins seen today are the remains of a castle that was later built on the site. Legend has it that just days before the fall of the fortress, some Cathars managed to escape with a secret treasure. This legend inspired conspiracy theories as well as some fictional works.

Great views to the mountains and valleys from Château de Montségur

STAGE 3
Montségur to Comus

Start	Montségur
Finish	Comus
Time	4hr 30min
Distance	16km
Total ascent	1120m
Total descent	875m

A short climb from Montségur is followed by a long steady descent. The second part of the stage takes you through a scenic gorge with towering walls. This is not a particularly demanding section and it will leave you enough time to relax in the afternoon.

Facilities Stage 3

4hr 30min		Comus	Le Silence du Midi (packed lunch)

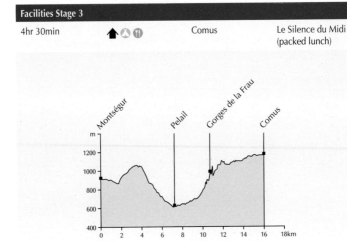

Looking back towards Montségur

Follow the GR signs through the village and go left through the archway shortly before reaching a stone trough. Walk alongside some gardens and go right uphill by a building with picnic benches to reach the D9. Go left and then keep immediately left through the car park. At the end of the car park take the track on the left. This area is also the village's campsite and for about €4 you can pitch your tent and have a shower (payable in the museum). A few minutes later, come to a track junction where you bear left. On reaching a tarmac road keep left. Shortly after go right on a track. Soon the track crosses over a stream on a bridge and continues as a footpath.

At the path junction go right. Ignore a path on the right and then take the path paved with rocks that curves uphill on the right. Ascend through forest scattered with moss-covered rocks.

Meet a surfaced track and keep left, then leave it to the right alongside a field. Soon you walk through woods again. After a short climb, reach a clearing with a great view back towards Château de Montségur which overlooks the village. Shortly after, there is a steep downhill section. This can get really muddy in the spring or after heavy rain. Ignore any path marked with an 'X' and follow the GR signs.

You will descend through forest for an hour or so alongside the rushing stream, crossing it a few times on rocks. The branches are thickly covered with moss in this fairytale forest.

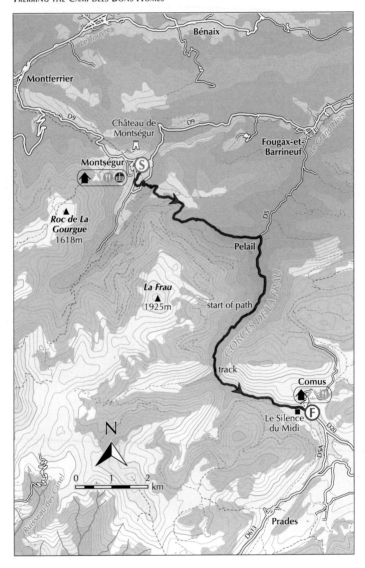

Walk between the sheer cliffs of the Frau gorge

The forest opens up and the path becomes a track just before you reach the tiny hamlet of **Pelail** (Hameau de Pelail, **2hr 30min**). Passing the houses, reach the D5. Go right, passing Aire de Repos de Pelail picnic site.

Follow the narrow tarmac lane, surrounded by towering mountains, for about 30min, entering **Gorges de la Frau**. The D5 road comes to an end and you climb the path next to a sheer rock wall. The Gorges de la Frau is a protected area. The beech-fir forest on limestone provides an important habitat for insects and birds.

Walk alongside the streambed of the Grand Hers, often near the rock wall in this lush gorge, for about 40min. When you reach a track by the information board about the area's wildlife, keep left. Follow the track for a further 40min, ignoring any other unmarked tracks. The track brings you out of the gorge and eventually becomes a tarmac road shortly before you arrive at **Comus**.

STAGE 4
Comus to Orlu

Start	Comus
Finish	Orlu
Time	8hr
Distance	28km
Total ascent	940m
Total descent	1270m

The landscape slowly changes. After passing the castle ruins in Montaillou, there is no shortage of fine views as you ascend through meadows. Be sure to leave early if you want to take the alternative route from Ascou, taking on La Forge d'Ascou and the mountain pass of Col de l'Osque before descending to Orlu. Fortunately from Ascou you can instead opt for a shorter, more direct route to Orlu.

From the D20 road go right, passing **Le Silence du Midi** (gîte, campsite). Follow the track signed towards Prades with the football pitch on your left.

Walk alongside meadows with some views of the mountains. At the track junction go right and then at La Fajole (1230m) path junction continue straight on. The GR107 is well signposted and easy to follow. The path becomes a track by a barn, where you arrive at **Prades (1hr)** after about an hour from Comus.

Continue straight on the tarmac road and follow the GR signs among the houses of Prades. Reach and cross the D613 near Font de le Cabaillère and head towards the cemetery.

Pass the cemetery and then follow the track away from Prades. Cross the stream on rocks and then curve left by a wooden cabin. Ascend through the woods with some views of nearby mountains when the trees peter out. Descend alongside grazing fields and meet a track and go left. Shortly after, reach a tarmac lane. Keep right and about 30min from Prades, arrive at **Montaillou (1hr 30min)**.

Follow the red and white signs through the village, passing a small local museum, a snack bar, a picnic area and a church. At **Château de Montaillou** (1332m, **1hr 45min**) go right to make a short detour to the castle ruins.

Facilities Stage 4

Time		Place	Accommodation
1hr	🍴	Prades	
1hr 30min	⬆🍴	Montaillou	La Caminada Vielha (B&B)
6hr	⬆🏕🍴	Sorgeat	Les Balcons de Sorgeat
6hr 20min	⬆	Ascou	Chambre d'Hôtes Le Belvédère
7hr 20min	🍴	Orgeix	
8hr	⬆🏕🍴	Orlu	Le Relais Montagnard (packed lunch)

Comus — Prades — Château de Montaillou — Col de Balaguès — Col de Pierre Blanche — Col d'Ijou de Sorgeat — Ascou — Porteille d'Orgeix — Orlu

(elevation profile, m vs km)

Approaching the small village of Prades, about an hour from Comus

43

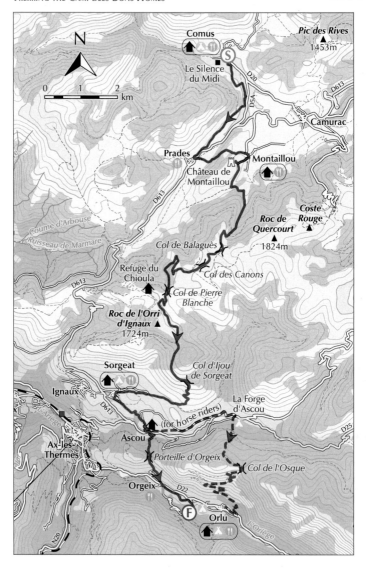

Château de Montaillou belonged to Bernard d'Alion, who sympathized with the Cathars. After the siege of Montségur (1244) the fortress was partially destroyed. Bernard d'Alion was condemned as a heretic and burnt at the stake in 1258. The castle was rebuilt and became a frontier fortress between the County of Foix and Aragon. However, the castle fell into disrepair after the Albigensian Crusade and in 1638, just like the Castle of Montségur, it was demolished following an order from Louis XIII.

From the ruins return to Château de Montaillou junction and continue on the path by a fountain (Font de Ribèlh). Descend with some mountain views and arrive at La Du Pichaca (1319m) junction. Go left on a track signed towards Col de Balaquès. Turn right uphill on the grassy path and shortly after, at Brulladou (1330m) junction, keep right on a path signed towards Col de Balaquès. Ascend through forest with a stream on your left down below. Cross a track and continue to climb. Ignore any other paths and go left at the junction. About 50min from Brulladou, arrive at **Col de Balaquès** (1670m, **3hr 20min**).

At this col the GR107 meets the GR7B, so both routes are therefore marked with red and white stripes. Go right and descend on the GR107 to **Col des Canons** (1610m). Continue straight on with some views of the nearby mountains. Walk through meadows with views over to Prades in the valley. The path becomes a mountain track, passing a spring. About 1hr from Col de Balaquès at **Col de Pierre Blanche** (1549m), continue straight on and, joining a track, keep right. A few minutes later at Pla de Lagarde (1605m) meet a track and go left. For about 20min follow the track on the mountainside with views dominated by mountains and meadows. Carry straight on at the junction and ignore unmarked paths.

At **Col d'ljou de Sorgeat** (1650m) leave the track to the left. Descend initially through forest, and then curve towards Sorgeat on the mountainside with some excellent views of the neighbouring mountains for about an hour before arriving on a tarmac lane. Go right, then a few minutes later turn left onto a track and walk alongside pastures. At a track junction keep right and descend to a tarmac road. Keep left and follow the red and white GR signs among the houses to **Sorgeat** junction (1050m, **6hr**) in front of the Mairie (town hall). Go left and skirt around a playground, following the tarmac lane that becomes a track at the edge of the village. Walk through forest, crossing a stream on a footbridge, and come to a surfaced road near a house. Go right and descend to **Ascou** (**6hr 20min**).

The GR107 route splits by Ascou Fontaine. The alternative route continues straight on and takes on **La Forge d'Ascou** and **Col de l'Osque** mountain pass before descending to Orlu. This route adds an additional 6.5km walking to the day. This variant is also suitable for horse riders.

Cross the Oriège river and follow it to Orlu, with spectacular landscapes all around

The other route, however, follows a shorter and more direct route. Go right downhill towards Orgeix and follow the red and white signs, passing a church. Cross a road and continue downhill on the track, passing some stone buildings and crossing the Lauze river over a bridge. At Fournit junction (930m) continue towards Orlu and, after passing some houses, walk through woods. At the next junction go right and from **Porteille d'Orgeix** (990m) zigzag downhill for about 15min to reach a tarmac road by a cemetery. Go left, and shortly after cross the D22 and then a stone bridge over the Oriège river. Turn left and follow the GR signs alongside the river Oriège on the wide path for about 20min to La Jonquiere (829m) junction. The GR107 continues to the right. However, if you have accommodation in Orlu, continue straight on for a further 10min to the centre. Walk through a campsite then cross the bridge to reach the centre of **Orlu**.

If you want a wider choice of accommodation you might want to visit the attractive spa town Ax-les-Thermes nearby. The town also has a train station, restaurants and shops. To spend a night in Ax-les-Thermes on reaching the D22 in Orgeix turn right and follow it to the spa town.

STAGE 5
Orlu to Mérens-les-Vals

Start	Orlu
Finish	Mérens-les-Vals
Time	5hr
Distance	17km
Total ascent	1045m
Total descent	735m

This is a short but nevertheless stunning stage. The long and constant but somehow easy climb through forest to Col de Joux is rewarded with stunning mountain views. After traversing a wide ridge, descend to Mérens-les-Vals with endless views of the valley. Don't miss the charming, ruined Saint-Pierre de Mérens church in the village.

Facilities Stage 5

5hr   Mérens-les-Vals Auberge du Nabre (packed lunch)

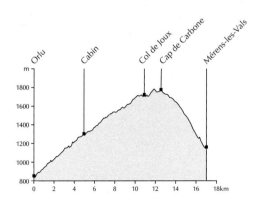

*Coll de Jou offers a fantastic panorama
back towards the deep valley below*

From Orlu take the Promenade Michel Peyre alongside the river, crossing the campsite to La Jonquiere (829m) junction, and go left on the track signed towards Mérens-les-Vals.

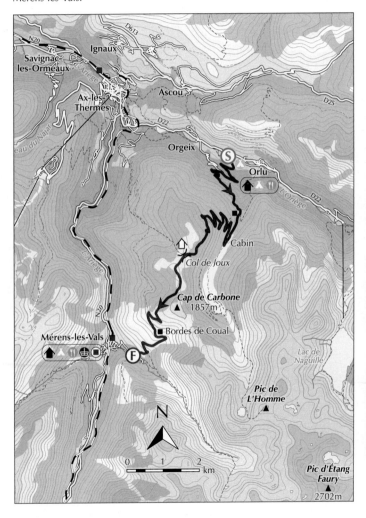

Follow the track uphill on the mountainside for about 30min to meet another track in a road bend. Keep left here. About 10min later turn right on a track and continue to ascend with some views down to the valley.

Meet another track and keep right. Ignoring any unmarked tracks, ascend with occasional views of the nearby mountains and of Orlu down below for another 30min and pass a building. Shortly after you can see a stream (Ruisseau de la Vallée d'Orgeix) down below on the left. Soon after the building, pass a **cabin** and then keep right on a grassy track that takes you above the cabin.

For the next 1hr 30min follow the track, snaking constantly but gradually uphill with countless switchbacks. Ignore any unmarked tracks and tracks marked with 'X'. The track becomes more rugged and narrows down to a path before emerging from the woods to a meadow at a col. Cross the meadow to the **Col de Joux** signpost (1702m, **3hr**). There is a small unmanned refuge/hut on the meadow near the woods. Towering mountains dominate the views and it is possible to make out the buildings of Ax 3 Domaines ski resort in the distance. Traverse the meadow to the trees. Walk among mighty tall pines and then descend to another meadow. Follow the wide ridge with some spectacular mountain views. About 30min from Col de Joux, descend to a junction with a signpost where you join a track at a bend, taking the right branch and ignoring another track joining immediately from the right.

Descend with some great views of the nearby mountains and the valley down below. Leave this track to the left near a cattle grid and continue to descend

The trail follows a wide mountain ridge for a while before it drops down towards Mérens

towards Mérens. At the path junction carry straight on towards a ramshackle house, **Bordes de Coual**, which you then pass below.

Go left through a gate and follow the path snaking downhill, ignoring any paths marked with an 'X'. Go sharply right and walk with the Ruisseau de Saint-Touret stream on your left. The path eventually becomes a surfaced road by the first house. Arrive at Mérens d'en Haut (1177m) junction. The GR10 and GR107 trails meet here. The next stage continues across the stream. To find your accommodation (if it is in Mérens) continue straight on downhill, crossing a road. Head towards the church tower and then down to the centre of **Mérens-les-Vals** (1040m, **5hr**).

The Romanesque church of **Saint-Pierre de Mérens** dates back to the 10th century, with the bell tower dating to around the 11th century. The village built around the church was an important stopover for travellers. In 1811 the church and the village were burnt down by the Spanish during the Spanish War of Independence (1808–1814).

The Romanesque church of Saint Pierre in Mérens

STAGE 6
Mérens-les-Vals to Porta

Start	Mérens-les-Vals
Finish	Porta
Time	9–10hr
Distance	25km
Total ascent	1750m
Total descent	1385m

The described variant is probably one of the most spectacular sections of the GR107 trail. Leave early, as the day starts with a demanding climb. Your efforts will be rewarded with rushing streams and rugged mountain views all the way up to Porteille des Bésines and through the Bésines valley. You can opt for the less demanding (winter/bad weather) variant that runs through the valley between Mérens-les-Vals and L'Hospitalet, shortening the walking hours on this section by 3hr 30min to 4hr.

From Mérens d'en Haut (1177m) junction you will be following a section that is marked as GR10 (sharing a route with the GR107) all the way to Refuge des Bésines. From Mérens d'en Haut junction follow the lane signed towards Refuge des Bésines.

Go over the bridge and shortly after turn left and up on the path, leaving the track and then eventually the village. Ascend among moss-covered rocks and soon notice warm water running down the path. This is coming from the nearby hot spring that you pass shortly. At the path junction go right and zigzag uphill. This is the beginning of the 3hr climb, with spectacular views of the rugged mountains. Soon you ascend alongside the rushing Nabre stream, crossing it several times and then curving right away from the stream where the steeper and more demanding climb starts.

> The **Mérens horse** is native to the upper valley of Ariège. Named after the village of Mérens-les-Vals, the small black mountain horse is known for its sure-footedness on mountain terrain, as well as for its endurance and hardiness.

4hr	🔼 🍽	Refuge des Bésines (manned refuge)
6hr 55min [1.5km off route]	🔼 ⛺ 🍽 ⊕ ⬛	L'Hospitalet prés-l'Andorre
8hr 40min [2km off route]	🔼 🍽 ⬛	Porte-Puymorens
9hr	⭕ 🔼 🍽 ⬛	Porta / Auberge du Campcardós (packed lunch)

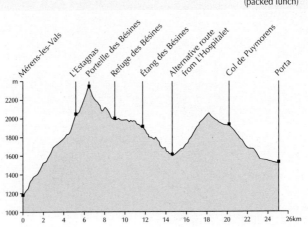

Traditionally, every June cattle, sheep and horses, including the Mérens breed, are moved to summer pastures at around 1500m where they will spend the summer months in a semi-wild state before returning to the valley in October. This tradition started to die out but it was reintroduced to the Ariège in 2000.

Another stream races down on rocks and you are surrounded by spectacular rugged mountains. After a little over 2hrs of steady climbing from the hot spring, reach a small tarn (**L'Estagnas**, **2hr 15min**). This picturesque place demands a short break. From the tarn there is another 30–40min steep climb to **Porteille des Bésines** (2333m, **2hr 55min**), with magnificent views back towards the Nabre

Pic de l'Etang
Rébenty
▲
2415m

Pyramide
de Lierbès
▲

Pic de Castille
▲

s pic de
lassis

de
be
4m

de
ecio'
9m

▲ 2633m

ANDORRA

Mérens-les-Vals

(winter variant)

Pic
d'Auriol ▲
2695m

Porteille
des Bésines
2333m

L'Estagnas

Étang des
Bésines

Refuge des
Bésines

Pic de
L'Homme
▲

Ruisseau du Nabre

Puig Pedros
▲

Puig de la
Coma d'Or
2825m

L'Hospitalet-
près-l'Andorre

Pic
Mercader
▲
2547m

2663m

Rec d'en Garcia

N320

Col de Puymorens

Map continues
on page 57

55

Head towards the mountain pass, Porteille des Bésines

valley. From the col descend, initially zigzagging downhill and then traversing a meadow scattered with rocks for about 45min to **Refuge des Bésines** (**4hr**).

Continue on the GR10 by the refuge building. Shortly after, at a path junction, the GR10 leaves the shared section. Go right and follow the GR107 downhill. Descend for about 30min, crossing a stream once on a wooden bridge and then a few more times on rocks, to **Étang des Bésines** (lake). Walk alongside the lake, passing a dam building at its western end and then an unmanned cabin. Follow the path, initially through forest and then alongside a stream with breathtaking views over the valley and L'Hospitalet. Zigzag downhill passing a waterfall and arrive at **L'Hospitalet** junction (**6hr 30min**), about 1hr 30min from the lake. The winter variant of the GR107 trail joins from the right from L'Hospitalet at this junction.

The winter variant goes through the village of **L'Hospitalet**, and you can see it from the normal route. According to legend a pilgrim on his way to Ax was caught in a terrible snow storm while descending from Col du Puymorens. In desperation, he killed his horse and tore out its insides. He then survived the storm in the animal's skin. To save other pilgrims from such an experience, he built a refuge on the spot where he nearly died. Nothing remains of this legendary refuge, but it is known that by the end of the first millennium the pass was a merchant route and there was a refuge for pilgrims. The current village was built around this legendary refuge.

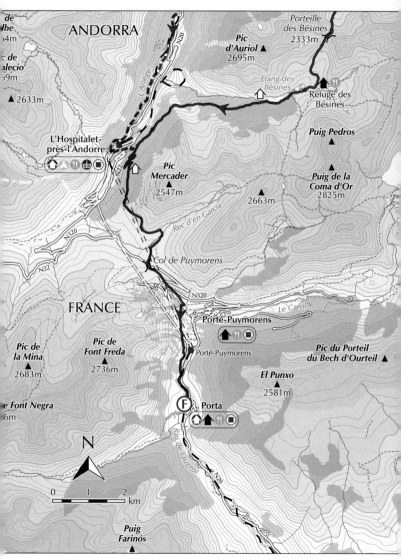

Spectacular scenery viewed from the steep climb after L'Estagnas

Continue straight on and climb on the mountainside for about 45min with views over the Ariège valley, passing some rather large water pipes supported by concrete columns. Pass an unmanned refuge and arrive on a track. Go right, and shortly after come to another track and carry straight on. There are red and white signs to follow. Meet another track and go right downhill. At the next junction go right and cross over a bridge near a pasture. Ignore the track on the left and follow the track down to the N320 road at **Col de Puymorens** (1915m, **8hr**).

Cross the road and walk through the car park and locate the signpost at the far end. After a short descent on a path, reach the road again. Cross it and continue downhill on its other side. Once more, reach and cross the road and continue to descend. At the path junction go right. Cross a stream on a bridge and by the signpost continue straight on the path signed for Porta. Follow the red and white signs, crossing a ski slope, and on reaching a track go right. A few minutes later, at a track junction, go right and follow the surfaced track alongside a river. Cross the bridge and then keep right on a track parallel to the busy road and railway to reach **Porta** (1510m, **9hr**). The Ax-les-Thermes and Porta-Puymorens section is the highest part of this Transpyrenean railway line that connects Foix and Puigcerdá. Therefore, it is possible to only walk the French part of the trail and take a train from Porta back to either Foix or Toulouse.

STAGE 7
Porta to Bellver de Cerdanya

Start	Porta
Finish	Bellver de Cerdanya
Time	10hr 30min
Distance	36km
Total ascent	1170m
Total descent	1660m

The stage starts with a steady climb through the Campcardós valley, with extensive views of rugged mountains, to reach Portella Blanca, the highest point of the entire trek. After crossing into Catalonia the scenery is just as spectacular. There are plenty of stream crossings and endless alpine meadows, and with some luck you might spot some marmots during the descent from Portella Blanca. This is a long day that can be divided into two by spending a night in the tiny hamlet of Viliella near the spectacular Molí de Salt waterfall. By doing this you have a short and easy day to Bellver de Cerdanya the next day. This obviously adds an extra day to your trip but allows you to explore the pretty town of Bellver de Cerdanya.

At Porta re-join the GR107, keeping left on Chemin du Campcardós with the river on your right. At Porta junction (1509m) continue by the river towards Portella Blanca. After the cattle grid cross the bridge to a car park with information boards and then follow the track alongside pastures. Pass an antenna and its building, and shortly after reach another track where you go left.

Ascend, initially on a track in the valley with rugged mountains all around. The track then narrows into a path and you cross a stream several times before reaching a small unmanned **refuge** building about 1hr 30min after leaving Porta.

From the refuge it will take about two hours of climbing to reach Portella Blanca. Ascend the narrow path, passing two tarns and crossing the stream several times on rocks. Traverse the rock-scattered meadow, with rugged mountains dominating the scenery all around, before the final zigzag up to **Portella Blanca**

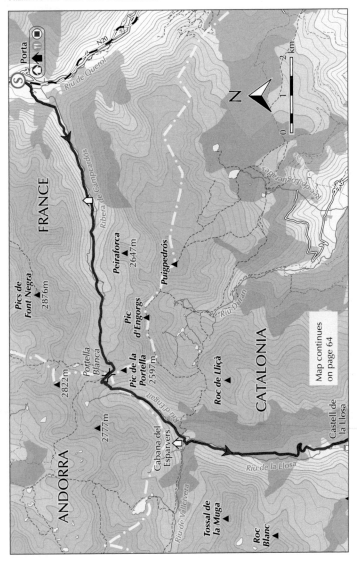

Map continues on page 64

62

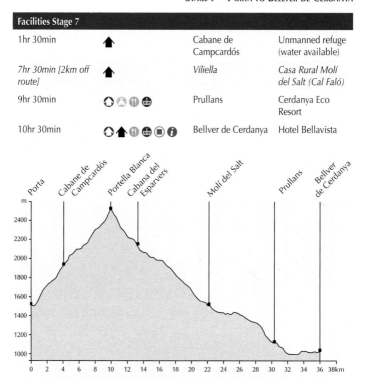

Facilities Stage 7			
1hr 30min	↑	Cabane de Campcardós	Unmanned refuge (water available)
7hr 30min [2km off route]	↑	*Viliella*	*Casa Rural Molí del Salt (Cal Faló)*
9hr 30min	⬡ △ 🍴 🏧	Prullans	Cerdanya Eco Resort
10hr 30min	⬡ ↑ 🍴 🏧 ◼ ℹ	Bellver de Cerdanya	Hotel Bellavista

(2517m, **3hr 30min**). France, Andorra and Catalonia meet at this point, which is also the highest point of the entire trek.

After crossing the 'border' you start to descend. The red and white signs are frequently painted on rocks and easy to follow. The path curves left and zigzags downhill towards the valley and a snaking stream. You might spot marmots as you descend towards the stream.

Marmots were reintroduced to the Pyrenees in 1948. They prefer the higher slopes between 1000 and 3200m. If you don't see them, you might hear the whistling noises they make to warn each other. They spend the summer months eating to build up fat for the winter when they will hibernate in their burrows for about seven months.

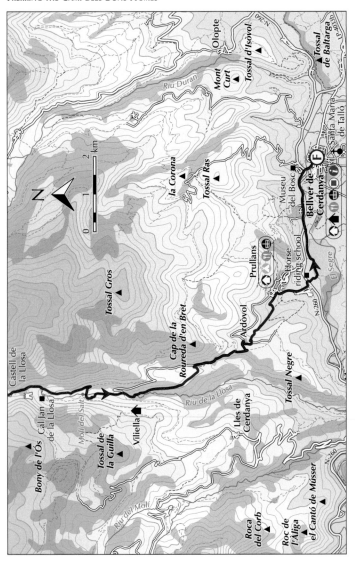

Hikers resting at Portella Blanca before continuing on the GR107 into Catalonia

You cross the rushing stream several times and descend alongside it. After descending for over an hour from Portella Blanca, walk through a meadow with an intersection where the GR11 and GR107 meet. Continue on the path signed for Cal Jan de la Llosa, straight on.

Shortly after cross another meadow with a small stone hut (**Cabana del Esparvers**). Reach a signpost and then, keeping left, drop down to the bridge. Cross over the bridge and then keep left on the GR107.

Walk through another meadow with the ruins of a house and a shrine. Follow the forest track snaking downhill near the Llosa river for about 1hr–1hr 15min (passing the ruins of **Castell de la Llosa**) to Cal Jan de la Llosa junction. **Cal Jan de la Llosa farm** is on the right on the other side of the river. Continue straight on alongside pastures. Leave the forest track to the right on a path going downhill to the Llosa river and the **Molí del Salt waterfall (7hr 30min)**.

If you would prefer to spend a night in Viliella, take the path on the right shortly after the waterfall. It leads to a track where you turn left. Follow this to the village. It is highly recommended that you pre-book your accommodation in Viliella.

After the border crossing, follow the well-waymarked path down the valley

To continue to Bellver de Cerdanya, ignore the path on the right and shortly after ignore another path on the right. That narrow overgrown path also leads to Viliella.

Descend near the river with some views of the houses of Viliella nestled on the hilltop. About 20min from the waterfall, reach and cross a tarmac road and continue straight on by the river. Keep left, crossing the river just before reaching a house. Shortly after cross the stream on a plank and then again on a bridge.

Reach and cross a track and continue straight on, parallel to a track. Go through a gate and walk alongside a fence. You have some great views of the Moixeró ridge, and you can see the houses of Lles de Cerdanya perched on a peak across the valley in the near distance. After a short downhill section, join a track near a gate.

Reach a road and turn right. Follow this quiet country lane for about 20min, ignoring other joining roads, to **Ardòvol**. Turn right downhill, passing some houses, and then leave the lane, going left on a forest track. Shortly after go left downhill on a path with a stream on your left.

Pass the allotments of the Eco resort and on reaching a track, go right downhill to Prullans. When the track splits keep left. This track becomes a tarmac road by the first house in **Prullans (9hr 30min)**. Follow the red and white signs among houses to a junction. Keep right downhill and follow the road down to the N-260. Cross over and the GR107 continues by the **horse riding school**. Ignore a track on the right. Pass a pen and keep left near the next building, then shortly after the narrow lane runs parallel to the N-260. After passing some houses reach and cross the N-260 and continue to the right, passing some industrial buildings roughly parallel to the N-260. Pass a hostel and arrive back on the N-260. Keep left and walk along the road to the Bellver de Cerdanya sign. Keep left and follow the red and white signs to the roundabout in **Bellver de Cerdanya (10hr 30min)**.

BELLVER DE CERDANYA

Wander the narrow cobbled streets of the old walled town of Bellver de Cerdanya, built on the rocky hilltop. Located on the border between Cerdanya and Urgell counties, the fortress had an important role of controlling the area at medieval times. In the old town you find a market square, a gothic church, a prison tower, and also a Spanish Civil War air raid shelter from the more recent past. There are some great views over the valley and town from the walls.

The Tourist Information Centre, near Santa Maria de Talló church, houses a small but interesting exhibition about the area and local life (Centre d'Interpretació del Parc Natural Cadí-Moixeró, tel +34 973510802, https://parcsnaturals.gencat.cat).

At the edge of the town there is also the less well-known but nevertheless fascinating Museu del Bosc (tel +34 680289997), where you can learn how the slopes of Moixeró were reforested. If you are interested in a visit, you need to pre-book it which you can do in the Tourist Information Centre.

STAGE 8
Bellver de Cerdanya to Bagà

Start	Bellver de Cerdanya
Finish	Bagà
Time	7hr
Distance	24km
Total ascent	1050m
Total descent	1195m

As you enter the Cadí-Moixeró area the landscape changes but continues to provide spectacular views. The route takes you alongside a river and then climbs through forest. The scenery is dominated by the remarkable rocky Moixeró ridge. There are two manned refuges where you can stop for refreshments before you start the descent to Bagà.

From the roundabout near the Hotel Bellavista, cross the bridge over the El Segre river and follow the red and white GR signs straight on to a small Tourist Office. Turn right onto Camí Talló by the map board and follow it to **Santa Maria de Talló church**.

Documented as an important place of worship since the 10th century, the **'Cathedral of Cerdanya'** is one of the finest example of Romanesque architecture in the area. The apse, covered by a barrel vault, is from the 11th century and the nave, divided into four parts and supported by semicircular pillars, is from the 13th century. The wooden polychrome carving of Madonna with Child is from the 12th century. You can admire the original ironwork on the wooden entrance door.

If you want to visit the church, ask for the key in the nearby tourist office. This also houses a small local museum.

After the church, pass Plaça de la Font and continue on Camí de l'Ingla, heading towards the mountains.

Facilities Stage 8		
20min	⬡ 🍴 ℹ️	Talló
2hr 50min	⬆️ 🍴	Refugi Cortals de l'Ingla
3hr 50min	⬆️ 🍴	Refugi Sant Jordi
7hr	⬡ ⛺ 🍴 🏧 ⬛ ℹ️	Bagà

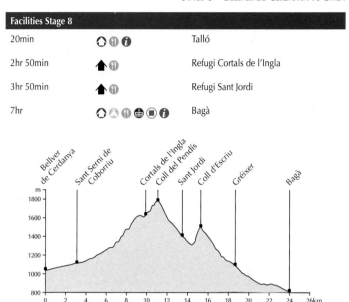

At the small Coborriu de Bellver (1080m) junction, keep right towards Vall d'Ingla and pass a fenced off waterworks area. About 10–15min from Santa Maria de Talló arrive at the 10th-century **Sant Serni de Coborriu church**.

> The small **church** has a single rectangular nave with a semicircular apse. Look out for the engraved head on the pillar next to the entrance door on the south wall.

Shortly after pass a large house and then follow the track in the Ingla river valley, passing Font de Capallá. After crossing the river, leave the track to the right to cross a narrow bridge and then arrive back on the track and keep right uphill. Arrive at **Font de l'Ingla** picnic site less than an hour after passing Sant Serni de Coborriu church.

Just after the picnic site go left on the path and cross the stream. Ascend on the narrow path near a house. Go through the meadow with some views of the nearby mountains. A few minutes later reach a track. Go right and shortly after

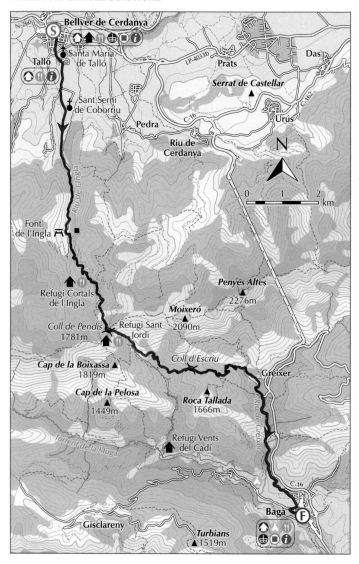

take the path on the left, uphill. Walk first through a meadow and then through forest, and reach and cross a track. Continue on its other side, uphill, and shortly after cross the track again. The views are dominated by pine-covered mountains.

Leaving the wide path, go left up on a narrow path through forest. When you reach the track go right, and a few metres later turn right uphill on a narrow path. Walk through a meadow, and reach and cross a tarmac road then climb to the **Refugi Cortals de l'Ingla (2hr 50min)**. Arrive at the refuge, about an hour from the picnic site.

There are some great views from the building. From the refuge, continue on the track signed towards Coll de Pendís with some great views of the Moixeró ridge. Leave the track to the right by a concrete reservoir. Walk through forest and then take the narrow path on the left uphill. This turn-off might only be marked with cairns (just before the wide path crosses a stream) and you may only see red markers to show the way.

Follow the forest path, occasionally crossing the stream, for about 20min and arrive at **Coll de Pendís** (1781m) junction. Keep left downhill through a gate and zigzag down on the rocky path for about 20–30min to **Refugi Sant Jordi**

Santa Maria de Talló church

An interesting carving of a face on the portal arch of Sant Serni de Coborriu church

(**3hr 50min**). Skirt around the building, and at Font del Faig junction keep left on the path signed towards Gréixer. Descend initially on the rocky mountainside with far-reaching views and then through forest.

Emerging from the forest, descend with views of the rocky ridge and of the Pendís valley below. After passing a house, the path widens. Go left up on a path and climb through forest for about 20min. It is a steep section, with the first glimpse of the magnificent Pedraforca mountain on the right. Reach a track by a signpost and go sharply left. Descend the stony track for about 30min, ignoring any unmarked tracks. Cross the stream twice, once on a bridge and then on rocks to **Gréixer** junction (**6hr**). Keep right and walk alongside grazing fields with the houses of Gréixer above you on the left.

Reach the BV4024 road. Turn right and follow it for nearly 4km (**about 1hr**) to a road junction to meet Avenida del Districte Forestal at the outskirts of **Bagà**. If you are not keen on walking along the road you can arrange a taxi (TaxiTrail: +34 686349857).

Bagà caters to tourists and hikers, with accommodation, shops and restaurants open throughout the year. However, you might prefer to carry on to Refugi Vents del Cadí, located farther along the trail. (This would shorten the next stage.) Continue on Avenida del Districte Forestal. Passing the Centre del Parc del Cadí-Moixeró, follow the lane for about 2km (**25min**). Then leave the tarmac lane to the right on a track and walk along the track for a further 2km to **Refugi Vents del Cadí**.

BAGÀ

It is worth spending some time exploring the narrow cobbled streets of the old town of Bagà.

Bagà was founded in the ninth century and because of its close proximity to the Pyrenees and the border it soon became an important town.

The layout of the town was designed in the 13th century. It is home to some fine Romanesque architecture such as the 12th-century Sant Esteve Church with an impressive bell tower and apse with frescos.

The covered market square, Plaça Porxada, has been in use since the 14th century and a traditional medieval market is held every summer. The building of the 10th-century Pinós Palace – which was the residence of Pinós barons – is home to the Cathar and Medieval Centre. For more information about the centre and its opening times, visit www.turismebaga.cat.

Breathtaking scenery in the Cadí-Moixeró mountain range near Refugi Sant Jordi

STAGE 9
Bagà to Gósol

Start	Bagà
Finish	Gósol
Time	7hr
Distance	24km
Total ascent	1250m
Total descent	700m

Enjoy endless views of Pedraforca, one of the most emblematic mountains of Catalonia, before arriving at the picturesque Gósol which inspired Picasso. This is an easy stage and should leave you plenty of time to explore the castle ruins in Gósol in the afternoon.

If you have been staying in Bagà you can shorten the distance by taking a taxi to Refugi Vents del Cadí.

From Bagà take Avenida del Districte Forestal, passing the Centre del Parc del Cadí-Moixeró. Follow the lane for about 2km (**25min**). Leave the tarmac lane to the right on a track and walk along the track for a further 2km to **Refugi Vents del Cadí (1hr)**.

From Refugi Vents del Cadí follow the track signed towards Gisclareny and Saldes, passing another parking area. Ignore the path on the right. Pass a ruined house and cross the river on a bridge. About 15min from the refuge, take the path on the left signed towards Sant Martí del Puig. Ascend to a path junction near a building. The route continues to the right, but first go left to make a short detour to **Sant Martí del Puig chapel**.

The small Romanesque **chapel** dates back to the 10th century. The building has a single nave covered with a barrel vault, and has been modified and rebuilt throughout the centuries. The parish was an independent parish, but from the 15th century it was documented as a diocese of Gisclareny.

Facilities Stage 9

1hr	⬆ 🍴	Refugi Vents del Cadí
7hr	⬆⬆🏕🍴⊕▣ℹ	Gósol
[1.5km off route]	⬆	*Refugi Molí de Gósol*

Descend from El Collell, following a narrow path above the Cerneres river valley

75

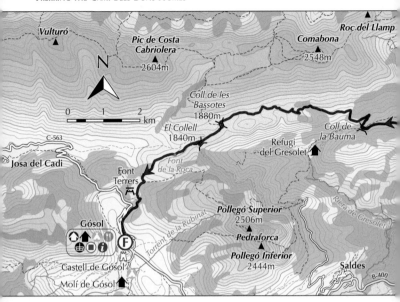

Returning to the junction from the chapel, continue straight on downhill and on reaching a track (Baga del Puig) keep right.

Follow the forest track, frequently marked with red and white signs with views of pine-covered mountains. At the junction keep left uphill and a few minutes later leave the track to the left uphill on a path signed towards Gósol. In the late spring and early summer, look out for orchids by the path. Reach and cross a track and continue uphill on its other side. Ignore the path to La Dou on the right and continue on a path signed towards Coll de la Bena.

Pass Font Vella and reach a track at **Coll de la Bena** (1437m, **3hr 15min**) about 1hr 45min from Sant Martí del Puig chapel. Take the forest track on the right, uphill. Follow this forest track for about 40min to **Coll de la Bauma** (**3hr 55min**), ignoring the green and white marked path on the left, and when the track splits take the left branch. At Coll de Bauma there is a picnic site near the track. At Coll de Bauma junction (1577m), continue on the track signed towards Gósol. Shortly after, ignore the green and white path on the right (this goes towards Comabona).

With some fantastic views to Pedraforca, follow the snaking track on the mountainside, ignoring any unmarked tracks, for about 1hr 30min.

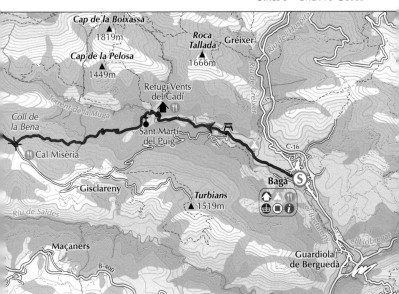

Great views towards the rugged peaks of Pedraforca from Gósol castle

Gósol castle ruins

At **Coll de les Bassotes** continue on the track but leave it about 10min later at **El Collell** (**5hr 35min**), to the right. Drop down on the grassy hillside to meet a path and keep left. Follow the narrow path on the mountainside, going mainly downhill with some amazing views of the valley. Pass **Font de la Roca** and about 20min later, at Torrent de la Coma dels Caners, keep right on a path signed towards Gósol (2.1km). Go through a gate near a reservoir and arrive on a track. Keep right and walk to **Font Terrers** picnic site (1625m, **6hr 25min**). Shortly after the picnic site, leave the track to the left. At the path junction go right. Descend through forest and soon the houses of **Gósol** appear. Reaching a track by a house, keep left, and follow the red and white signs to the main square.

GÓSOL

Gósol castle ruins are only a short stroll from the village square. The most prominent ruin in the old walled town is the 11th-century Romanesque Santa Maria church. This was only abandoned at the beginning of the 20th century when a new church was built in the village.

In the summer of 1906 Picasso and his mistress, Fernande Olivier, spent several weeks in Gósol. The landscape and people of Gósol, as well as his lover, gave him plenty of inspiration for his work during that time. The building that housed the inn where he stayed is on the main square.

STAGE 10
Gósol to Berga

Start	Gósol
Finish	Santuari de Queralt, Berga
Time	9hr, plus 45min to descend to Berga
Distance	29km, plus 3km to Berga
Total ascent	1330m
Total descent	1605m

From Gósol, make your way through some hamlets before the first steep climb and then traverse on mountainsides near striking rock walls to pass the abandoned village of Peguera. The last leg takes you through meadows. After the final climb, the GR107 comes to an end at the Santuari de Queralt above Berga. The last stage of the GR107 is long but you can divide it into two shorter days by spending a night near Peguera. (Note that the only accommodation in the Peguera area is about 4km off the trail so you might want to organize a pick up.)

From the roundabout at the outskirts of Gósol take the track parallel to the B-400 road and follow it, ignoring any joining tracks. About 10min from Gósol, pass Cap de la Creu peak and then keep right towards Sorribes. Go through the meadow and descend towards the houses.

Descend, crossing a stream on rocks, and then keep left on a track slightly uphill and parallel to B-400 to meet a tarmac lane. Go right and follow the signs among the houses of Sorribes and pass Sant Francesc de Sorribes church. Look out for the red and white sign on a lamp post and go left on the path on the grassy hillside. Shortly after descend through woods, crossing a stream, and then walk parallel to the B-400 road again. Keep right and about 20–30min from Sorribes, descend the lane to **L'Espà** (**1hr**, hotel, bus).

Walk through houses and then take the path to the right near Sant Andreu church and pass some more houses. Descend keeping left on a wider path after the electricity pylon, and shortly after cross a stream on rocks. Keep left by **La**

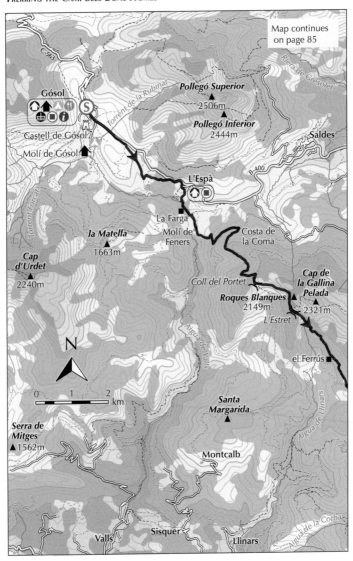

Map continues
on page 85

C-563

Gósol

Torrent de la Rubinat

Pollegó Superior
▲2506m

Pollegó Inferior
2444m

Saldes

Castell de Gósol
Molí de Gósol

S

L'Espà

B-400

Torrent Forcat

La Farga

Molí de Feners

Costa de
la Coma

la Matella
▲1663m

*Cap
d'Urdet*
▲2240m

Coll del Portet

Roques Blanques
2149m

L'Estret

*Cap de
la Gallina
Pelada*
▲2321m

Aigua de Valls

N

0   1   2
km

el Ferrús

*Santa
Margarida*
▲

Aigua de Llinars

*Serra de
Mitges*
▲1562m

Montcalb

Valls   Sisquer   Llinars

Aigua de la Corba

Riera de Gresolet

82

Facilities Stage 10			
1hr	⭗ ▣	L'Espà	
5hr 30min [5km off route]	▲	Peguera	*Cal Barbut (rural hotel – allow extra time or arrange a pickup)*
9hr	🍴	Santuari de Queralt	
9hr 45min	⭗ 🍴 ⊜ ▣ ⓘ	Berga	

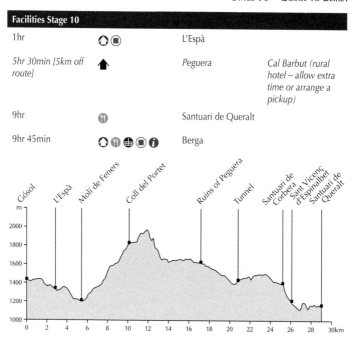

Farga farmhouse and ignore any unmarked paths. You can hear the sound of the rushing Aigua de Valls stream from behind the farmhouse.

At the junction take the path to the right signed towards Peguera (12.4km). Pass a house, and follow the path alongside the river. Reach a track at **Molí de Feners**. Keep right and cross a stream. At the next signpost, also named Molí de Feners, go left uphill on a track and pass a barn.

Keep left uphill on a wide path signed towards Peguera (11.3km). There is a view of Pedraforca on the left where there is an opening in the forest canopy. At the clearing, keep on the right-hand side and then ascend through forest, reaching a track where you go left.

Shortly after, at **Costa de la Coma**, take the path initially parallel to the track on the right-hand side. Ascend – occasionally steeply – for nearly an hour through forest then reach a track and go right. Look back to have a last glimpse of Pedraforca before you continue. Locate the signpost at **Coll del Portet** (1828m,

83

Last glimpse of Pedraforca at Coll del Portet

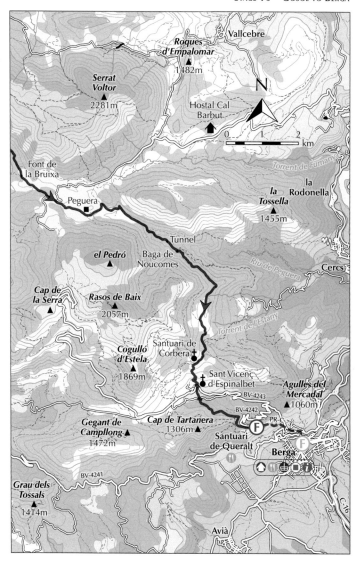

From Coll del Portet, follow the trail by the cliffs below Gallina Pelada and towards Ferrús

3hr 10min) and keep left on the grassy mountainside signed towards Peguera (8.5km). Follow the signs on rocks heading towards the rocky mountain.

Walk alongside the towering cliffs below the magnificent **Cap de la Gallina Pelada**. Descend for about 1hr 30min, often steeply and swinging close to the rock face several times, and then through forest.

Pass the ruins of a house and shortly after, come to a wide path and go left. At **Font de la Bruixa** take the second track from the left, signed towards Peguera (2.4km). On reaching a surfaced lane at Portell dels Terrers go left downhill and a few minutes later take the track on the right. Soon the remains of the abandoned houses of **Peguera (5hr 30min)** come into view, scattered on the hillside. You can stay in the rural accommodation that is about 5km off the route from the abandoned village of Peguera, but you can arrange a pick up. Follow the track to a junction by the old cemetery and carry straight on, passing some ruined houses and a spring.

After **coal mining** petered out in the area in the 1930s Peguera's inhabitants made a living by logging and cultivating, but the village was abandoned by the early 1960s.

At Font del Coix track junction, keep slightly right downhill. There are further ruins near the track. When the track splits take the left branch. At Picos del Moreta continue on the track downhill. About 30min from Peguera, at La Planelleta, take the path on the right downhill. Cross a rocky gorge and then continue uphill on the other side. Cross a bridge and shortly after go through a short **tunnel**.

At **Baga de Noucomes** take the path to the right and uphill, signed towards Queralt (8km). Follow the path on the mountainside for about 30min, with some views of the rugged mountains. Emerging from the forest, go through a small clearing, ignoring a track on the left. Keep left by the farmhouse and descend, ignoring a path on the left. Turó del Serretal peak with antennas is on your left. At the junction take the gravel track downhill signed towards Queralt (4.4km). A few minutes later, at Plans de Corbera track junction, go left and follow the red and white signs through the meadow with **Santuari de Corbera** and a farmhouse on a hillside to your right. You need to look out for the signs as other paths cross the meadow.

Shortly after, take the narrow path to the left downhill. Zigzag downhill for a few minutes with views over the valley to a path junction. Here bear right and pass a house and **Sant Vicenç d'Espinalbet church**. Turn left by the Espinalbet sign. The slightly overgrown path takes you below the houses and then down

The abandoned village of Peguera

A great panorama over Berga from Queralt

to a track. Go right and reach a tarmac road where you keep left. Shortly after leave the tarmac road to the right on a narrow surfaced road. Pass some houses and arrive on a tarmac road and go left. Leave the road to the right on a path and after crossing a stream, start the last ascent. Climb some big stone steps and at Baga de Cal Pere Sastre junction, go left and slightly downhill. The sanctuary is teasingly visible. On reaching a track go left, and shortly after arrive at **Santuari de Queralt (9hr)** where the Camí dels Bons Homes trail ends (or starts).

SANTUARI DE QUERALT

The sanctuary and its annex that today is a restaurant but used to be the sanctuary's inn and the nearby church of La Cueva make up of the Queralt complex. There was sanctuary positioned on the hill since the 14th century but the current church built in Renaissance style during 18th century was badly damaged during the Civil War and several restoration works were carried out during the following decades.

The town centre is a further 3km away. You can get to Berga from the Santuari de Queralt by following the PR-C 73 trail, marked with yellow and white. Descend the steps to the large parking area and then take the PR-C 73 path. Descend with views towards the town. Reach and cross the BV-4242 road and take the right branch of Balcó de Berguedà road going uphill. Where it forks follow the yellow and white signs to the left. In the bend of the road the trail continues as a path and leads to a road. Keep right and arrive on the BV-4241. Cross over the road and continue downhill, and follow Carrer de la Pinsania to the Convent de Sant Francesc in **Berga**.

BERGA

Berga was founded in the 12th century around the castle that still stands above the town was initially built. Throughout the centuries several wars affected the area and the town only recovered when industrializations began. Today the town's proximity to the mountains enables visitors to enjoy a range of outdoor activities. A bus service connects Berga with Barcelona and Puigcerdá from where you can start your journey back home.

APPENDIX A
Useful contacts and information

Useful websites

www.camidelsbonshomes.com

www.chemindesbonshommes.com

www.ariegepyrenees.com

www.pyrenees-ariegeoises.com

www.ariege.com

www.tourism-mediterraneanpyrenees.com

www.visitpirineus.com

www.catalunya.com

www.editorialalpina.com

www.cerdanya.org

www.elbergueda.cat

Tourist offices

Foix tourist office
29 Rue Théophile Delcassé, 09000
Foix, France
tel +33 561651212
www.foix-tourisme.com

Ax-les-Thermes tourist office
6 Av. Théophile Delcassé, 09110 Ax-les-
Thermes, France
tel +33 561646060
www.pyrenees-ariegeoises.com

Bellver de Cerdanya tourist office
Plaça Sant Roc, 25720 Bellver de
Cerdanya, Lleida, Spain
tel +34 973510229

Cadí-Moixeró Natural Park information
centre
Camí Talló, 5-23, 25721 Bellver de
Cerdanya, Lleida, Spain
tel +34 973510802
http://parcsnaturals.gencat.cat/cadi

Bagà tourist office
Carrer Pujada al Palau, 08695 Bagà,
Barcelona, Spain
tel +34 619746099
www.turismebaga.com/baga/

Gósol tourist office
Pl. Major, 1, 25716 Gósol, Lleida, Spain
tel +34 973370055
centremuntanya@gosol.ddl.net

Berga tourist office
Ctra. C-16, Km.96,200, 08600 Berga,
Barcelona, Spain
tel +34 654125696
www.elbergueda.cat

Accommodation

www.booking.com

www.gites-de-france.com

www.gites-refuges.com

www.airbnb.co.uk

www.hotelscombined.co.uk

www.travelsupermarket.com

Transport

Air

www.jet2.com

www.vueling.com

www.easyjet.com

www.britishairways.com

www.ryanair.com

www.skyscanner.net

Public transport
www.tisseo.fr (Toulouse)

Trains
www.thetrainline.com

www.raileurope.com

www.sncf.com (French)

www.renfe.com (Spanish)

Buses
www.mestrajets.lio.laregion.fr (French)

www.alsa.com (Spanish)

Taxi
Taxi Trail (on the Spanish sections)
tel +34 686349857
info@taxitrail.com
www.taxitrail.com

Taksi Trigotel: +34 630103225

Luggage transfer
Taxi Trail (on the Spanish sections)
tel +34 686349857
info@taxitrail.com
www.taxitrail.com

APPENDIX B

Accommodation

The following list details accommodation in sequential order. The number of places and type of accommodation on offer, and dates when open, are given where known. Further details may be obtained from the various tourist offices. Additions or alterations to the list would be welcomed by the authors.

Stage	Name	Type	Facilities	Open
1	Hotel Lons, Foix	⬭	24 rooms	All year
1	Auberge Le Léo de Foix, Foix	⬭	Rooms	All year
1	Camping La Roucateille, Foix	◯	Pitches, bungalows	All year
2	Gîte d'Etape de Roquefixade, Roquefixade	⬆	3 rooms and 1 dormitory with 6 beds	All year
2	Le Presbytère de Montferrier, Montferrier	⬆	Rooms	All year
3	La maison sous le château, Monségur	⬆	4 rooms	March to November
3	Gîtes Chez Luis (Macerou), Monségur	⬆	Rooms	All year
3	Camping de Monségur (municipal), Monségur	◯	Pitches	May to September
4	Le Silence du Midi, Comus	⬆ / ◯	Gîtes, safari tents and pitches	All year
4	Gîte d'étape Le Presbytère, Comus	⬆	Gîte, 7 rooms	All year
4	La Caminada Vielha, Montaillou	⬆	Rooms	All year
4	Refuge Chioula	⬆	Dormitory rooms with 4–10 places	All year
4	Camping Municipal La Prade, Sorgeat	◯	Pitches	April to November
4	Gîte Family House Ignaux	⬆	Rooms and dormitory with 8 places	All year

⭕ hotel 🔺 gîte/chambres d'hôtes/refuge Ⓐ campsite

Tel	Web/email	Comments
+33 534092800	www.hotel-lons-foix.com	
+33 561650904	www.leodefoix.fr	
+33 561640592	https://camping-roucateille.com	
+33 534140448	www.gite-etape-roquefixade.com	
+33 646560733	www.gites-de-france-ariege.com/location-Gite-Montferrier-Ariege-09G10413.html	
+33 688743964	www.lamaisonsouslechateau.com	
+33 534665774	www.ariegemontsegur.com	
+33 0561011027	www.montsegur.fr/services/hebergements	Contact the Museum Archéologique at 32 rue du village, Montségur
+33 468203626	www.lesilencedumidi.com/fr	
+33 468203369	www.gites-comus.com	
+33 953609584	www.lacaminadavielha.com	
+33 561640697	www.refugeduchioula.com/acces_refuge-chioula_ariegepyrenees.php	Manned mountain refuge
+33 630360898	www.camping-ariege-sorgeat.fr/camping	
+33 611171153	www.familyhouseignaux.com	650m off route near Sorgeat

Stage	Name	Type	Facilities	Open
4	Balcons de Sorgeat, Sorgeat	▲	Rooms	All year
4	Le Belvédère, Ascou	▲	Rooms	All year
4	La Forge d'Ascou	▲	Rooms and dormitory	All year
5	Le Relais Montagnard, Orlu	▲	Rooms and dormitory	All year
5	Camping d'Orlu, Orlu	⊘	Pitches and cottages	April to November
6	Auberge du Nabre, Mérens-les-Vals	▲	Rooms and dormitory	All year
6	Camping de Mérens	⊘	Pitches	All year
6	Refuge des Bésines	▲	Dormitory with 16 places	Closed in the winter
6	Hôtel du Puymorens	○	Rooms	All year
7	Le Campcardós, Porta	○	Rooms	All year
7	Gîte Équilibre, Porta	▲	Rooms	All year
7	Casa rural Molí del Salt (Cal Faló), Viliella	▲	Rooms	All year
7	Cerdanya Eco Resort, Prullans	○ ⊘	Rooms, apartments, bungalows, pitches	All year
8	Alberg la Bruna, Bellver de Cerdanya	▲	Rooms	All year
8	Hotel Bellavista, Bellver de Cerdanya	○	Rooms	All year
8	Hotel Bon Repòs, Bellver de Cerdany	○	Rooms	All year
8	Hotel Cal Rei de Talló, Talló	○	Rooms	All year
8	Refugi Cortals de l'Ingla	▲	Dormitory with 22 beds	May to November

Tel	Web/email	Comments
+33 612434821	www.balconsdesorgeat.fr	
+33 561640440	www.chambre-dhote-ariege.com	
+33 561646006	www.gite-restaurant-ascou.fr	3km off route on the alternative variant
+33 602085353	www.lerelaismontagnard-orlu.fr	
+33 561643009	www.camping-chalets-orlu.com	
+33 561018936	www.aubergedunabre.com	
+33 561028540	www.camping.merenslesvals.fr	2km off the main route, along the winter variant
+33 988773528	https://refugedesbesines.ffcam.fr	Manned refuge
+33 561052003	www.hoteldupuymorens.fr	In L'Hospitalet-près-l'Andorre on the winter variant
+33 468303890	www.aubergeducampcardos.com	
+33 642506324	www.equi-libre.fr	
+34 677262166	www.molidelsalt.com	In Viliella, 2km off route (alternative stopover)
+34 973510260	www.cerdanyaecoresort.com	
+34 677262166	www.alberglabruna.com	
+34 973510000	www.bellavistabellver.cat	
+34 973511243	www.bonreposhotel.com/es	
+34 609681979	www.hotelcalreidetallo.com	
+34 686 693 305	www.centralderefugis.com/product/refugi-cortals-de-lingla	Manned refuge

Stage	Name	Type	Facilities	Open	
8	Refugi Sant Jordi	▲	Dormitory with 36 beds	All year	
9	Refugi Vents del Cadí	▲	Rooms	All year	
9	Hostal Cal Batista, Bagà	⬡	Rooms	All year	
9	Camping Bastareny, Bagà	⬡	Pitches	All year	
9	Refugi del Gresolet	▲	Dormitory	May to October	
10	Hostal Cal Franciscó, Gósol	▲	Rooms	All year	
10	Cadí Vacances, Gósol	⬡	Bungalows, pitches	All year	
10	Refugi Molí de Gósol	▲	Dormitory	All year	
10	Hostal Cal Barbut	▲	Rooms	All year	
10	Camping Fontfreda	⬡	Pitches	All year	

Tel	Web/email	Comments
+34 619239860	www.refugisantjordi.com	Manned refuge
+34 938029227	www.ventsdelcadi.com	On route outside Bagà
+34 938244126	www.calbatista.es	
+34 938244420	www.campingbastareny.com	
+34 633106799	www.refugidelgresolet.com	2.5km off route near Coll de Bauma
+34 973370075	www.cal-francisco.com	
+34 636 066 465	www.cadivacances.com	
+34 636564310	www.molidegosol.com	1.5km off route near Gósol
+34 636449406	www.calbarbut.com	5.5km off route near Peguera (pick up offered)
+34 659764911	www.campingfontfreda.com	1.5km off route near Espinalbet

APPENDIX C

Glossary

French	Catalan	Spanish	English
bonjour	bon dia	buenos días	good morning
bon après-midi (only as goodbye)	bona tarda	buenos tardes	good afternoon
salut	hola	hola	hello
station de bus	estació d'autobusos	estación de autobúses	bus station
arrêt de bus	parada d'autobús	parada de autobús	bus stop
gare	estació de tren	estación de tren	railway station
train	tren	tren	train
bus	autobús	autobús	bus
voiture	cotxe	coche	car
horaire	horaris	horarios	timetable
billet	bitllet	billete	ticket
camping	càmping	cámping	campsite
gîte	alberg/hostal	albergue/hostal	guesthouse/hostel
auberge	alberg	albergue	lodge/guesthouse
chambre	habitació	habitación	room
tourisme rural	turisme rural	turismo rural	rural tourism
camping-car	autocaravana	caravana	campervan
tente	tenda	tienda	tent
abeilles	abelles	abejas	bees
cheval	cavall	caballo	horse
chien	gosso	perro	dog
vache	vaca	vaca	cow
église	església	iglesia	church
monastère	monastir	monasterio	monastery
école	escola	escuela	school
chapelle	capella	capilla	chapel
château	castell	castillo	castle
marché	mercat	mercado	market
supermarché	supermercat	supermercado	supermarket
ouvrir	obert	abierto	open
fermé	tancat	cerrado	closed
mairie	ajuntament	ayuntamiento	town hall
rue	carrer	calle	street
office de tourisme	oficina de turisme	oficina de turismo	tourist office
route	carretera	carretera	road
maison	casa	casa	house

French	Catalan	Spanish	English
ferme	masia	granja	farmhouse
petit-déjeuner	esmorzar	desayuno	breakfast
déjeuner	dinar	almuerzo	lunch
dîner	sopar	cena	dinner/supper
eau	aigua	agua	water
eau potable	bebent aigua	agua potable	drinking water
bière	cervesa	cerveza	beer
vin	vi	vino	wine
fromage	formatge	queso	cheese
café	cafè	cafe	coffee
pain	pa	pan	bread
élévation	elevació	elevación	elevation
danger	perill	peligro	danger
refuge	refugi	refugio	refuge
entrée	entrada	entrada	entrance
sortie	sortida	salida	exit
montagne	muntanya	montaña	mountain
gorge/ravin	gorg, barranc	barranco	ravine
vallée	vall	valle	valley
rivière	riu, riera	río	river
ruisseau	torrent, sot	torrente	stream
cascade	salt, cascada	cascada	waterfall
col	coll	coll	col
pic	puig	pico	peak
sommet	cim	cima	summit
barrage	presa	represa	dam
réservoir	pantà, embassament	embalse	reservoir
route	ruta, recorregud	ruta, recorrido	route
chemin	sendero, camí	sendero, camino	trail, path
grotte	cova	cueva	cave
carte	mapa	mapa	map
forêt	bosc	bosque	forest
privée	privat	privado	private
pont	pont	puente	bridge
fontaine/source	font	fuente	spring
randonneur	excursionista	excursionista	hiker
urgence	emergència	emergencia	emergency
feu	foc	fuego	fire
ambulance	ambulància	ambulancia	ambulance
pompiers	bombers	bomberos	fire brigade
police	policia	policía	police

DOWNLOAD THE GPX FILES

All the routes in this guide are available for download from:

www.cicerone.co.uk/1223/GPX

as standard format GPX files. You should be able to load them into most online GPX systems and mobile devices, whether GPS or smartphone. You may need to convert the file into your preferred format using a conversion programme such as gpsvisualizer.com or one of the many other such websites and programmes.

When you follow this link, you will be asked for your email address and where you purchased the guidebook, and have the option to subscribe to the Cicerone e-newsletter.

www.cicerone.co.uk

LISTING OF CICERONE GUIDES

BRITISH ISLES CHALLENGES, COLLECTIONS AND ACTIVITIES
Great Walks on the England Coast Path
Map and Compass
The Big Rounds
The Book of the Bivvy
The Book of the Bothy
The Mountains of England and Wales:
Vol 1 Wales
Vol 2 England
The National Trails
Walking the End to End Trail

SHORT WALKS SERIES
Short Walks Hadrian's Wall
Short Walks in the Lake District: Keswick, Borrowdale and Buttermere
Short Walks in the Lake District: Windermere Ambleside and Grasmere
Short Walks in the Lake District: Coniston and Langdale
Short Walks in Arnside and Silverdale
Short Walks in Nidderdale
Short Walks in Northumberland: Wooler, Rothbury, Alnwick and the coast
Short Walks on the Malvern Hills
Short Walks in Cornwall: Falmouth and the Lizard
Short Walks in Cornwall: Land's End and Penzance
Short Walks in the South Downs: Brighton, Eastbourne and Arundel
Short Walks in the Surrey Hills
Short Walks Winchester
Short Walks in Pembrokeshire: Tenby and the south
Short Walks on the Isle of Mull
Short Walks on the Orkney Islands

SCOTLAND
Ben Nevis and Glen Coe
Cycling in the Hebrides
Cycling the North Coast 500
Great Mountain Days in Scotland
Mountain Biking in Southern and Central Scotland
Mountain Biking in West and North West Scotland
Not the West Highland Way Scotland
Scotland's Best Small Mountains
Scotland's Mountain Ridges
Scottish Wild Country Backpacking
Short Walks in Dumfries and Galloway
Skye's Cuillin Ridge Traverse
The Borders Abbeys Way
The Great Glen Way

The Great Glen Way Map Booklet
The Hebridean Way
The Hebrides
The Isle of Mull
The Isle of Skye
The Skye Trail
The Southern Upland Way
The West Highland Way
West Highland Way Map Booklet
Walking Ben Lawers, Rannoch and Atholl
Walking in the Cairngorms
Walking in the Pentland Hills
Walking in the Scottish Borders
Walking in the Southern Uplands
Walking in Torridon, Fisherfield, Fannichs and An Teallach
Walking Loch Lomond and the Trossachs
Walking on Arran
Walking on Harris and Lewis
Walking on Jura, Islay and Colonsay
Walking on Rum and the Small Isles
Walking on the Orkney and Shetland Isles
Walking on Uist and Barra
Walking the Cape Wrath Trail
Walking the Corbetts
Vol 1 South of the Great Glen
Vol 2 North of the Great Glen
Walking the Galloway Hills
Walking the John o' Groats Trail
Walking the Munros
Vol 1 — Southern, Central and Western Highlands
Vol 2 — Northern Highlands and the Cairngorms
Winter Climbs in the Cairngorms
Winter Climbs: Ben Nevis and Glen Coe

NORTHERN ENGLAND ROUTES
Cycling the Reivers Route
Cycling the Way of the Roses
Hadrian's Cycleway
Hadrian's Wall Path
Hadrian's Wall Path Map Booklet
Pennine Way Map Booklet
The Coast to Coast Cycle Route
The Coast to Coast Walk
The Coast to Coast Map Booklet
The Pennine Way
Walking the Dales Way
The Dales Way Map Booklet

LAKE DISTRICT
Bikepacking in the Lake District
Cycling in the Lake District
Great Mountain Days in the Lake District
Joss Naylor's Lakes, Meres and Waters of the Lake District

Lake District Winter Climbs
Lake District:
High Level and Fell Walks
Low Level and Lake Walks
Mountain Biking in the Lake District
Outdoor Adventures with Children — Lake District
Scrambles in the Lake District —
North
South
Trail and Fell Running in the Lake District
Walking The Cumbria Way
Walking the Lake District Fells —
Borrowdale
Buttermere
Coniston
Keswick
Langdale
Mardale and the Far East
Patterdale
Wasdale
Walking the Tour of the Lake District

NORTH—WEST ENGLAND AND THE ISLE OF MAN
Cycling the Pennine Bridleway
Isle of Man Coastal Path
The Lancashire Cycleway
The Lune Valley and Howgills
Walking in Cumbria's Eden Valley
Walking in Lancashire
Walking in the Forest of Bowland and Pendle
Walking on the Isle of Man
Walking on the West Pennine Moors
Walking the Ribble Way
Walks in Silverdale and Arnside

NORTH—EAST ENGLAND, YORKSHIRE DALES AND PENNINES
Cycling in the Yorkshire Dales
Great Mountain Days in the Pennines
Mountain Biking in the Yorkshire Dales
The Cleveland Way and the Yorkshire Wolds Way
The Cleveland Way Map Booklet
The North York Moors
Trail and Fell Running in the Yorkshire Dales
Walking in County Durham
Walking in Northumberland
Walking in the North Pennines
Walking in the Yorkshire Dales:
North and East
South and West
Walking St Cuthbert's Way
Walking St Oswald's Way and Northumberland Coast Path

DERBYSHIRE, PEAK DISTRICT AND MIDLANDS

Cycling in the Peak District
Dark Peak Walks
Scrambles in the Dark Peak
Walking in Derbyshire
Walking in the Peak District — White Peak East
Walking in the Peak District — White Peak West

WALES AND WELSH BORDERS

Cycle Touring in Wales
Cycling Lon Las Cymru
Great Mountain Days in Snowdonia
Hillwalking in Shropshire
Mountain Walking in Snowdonia
Offa's Dyke Path
Offa's Dyke Map Booklet
Scrambles in Snowdonia
Snowdonia: 30 Low-level and Easy Walks
— North
— South
The Cambrian Way
The Pembrokeshire Coast Path
Pembrokeshire Coast Path Map Booklet
The Snowdonia Way
The Wye Valley Walk
Walking Glyndwr's Way
Walking in Carmarthenshire
Walking in Pembrokeshire
Walking in the Brecon Beacons
Walking in the Forest of Dean
Walking in the Wye Valley
Walking on Gower
Walking the Severn Way
Walking the Shropshire Way
Walking the Wales Coast Path

SOUTHERN ENGLAND

20 Classic Sportive Rides in South East England
20 Classic Sportive Rides in South West England
Cycling in the Cotswolds
Mountain Biking on the North Downs
Mountain Biking on the South Downs
Suffolk Coast and Heath Walks
The Cotswold Way
The Cotswold Way Map Booklet
The Kennet and Avon Canal
The Lea Valley Walk
The North Downs Way
North Downs Way Map Booklet
The Peddars Way and Norfolk Coast Path
The Pilgrims' Way
The Ridgeway National Trail
The Ridgeway Map Booklet
The South Downs Way
The South Downs Way Map Booklet
The Thames Path
The Thames Path Map Booklet
The Two Moors Way

Two Moors Way Map Booklet
Walking Hampshire's Test Way
Walking in Cornwall
Walking in Essex
Walking in Kent
Walking in London
Walking in Norfolk
Walking in the Chilterns
Walking in the Cotswolds
Walking in the Isles of Scilly
Walking in the New Forest
Walking in the North Wessex Downs
Walking on Dartmoor
Walking on Guernsey
Walking on Jersey
Walking on the Isle of Wight
Walking the Dartmoor Way
Walking the Jurassic Coast
Walking the Sarsen Way
Walking the South West Coast Path
South West Coast Path Map Booklet
— Vol 1: Minehead to St Ives
— Vol 2: St Ives to Plymouth
— Vol 3: Plymouth to Poole
Walks in the South Downs National Park
Cycling Land's End to John o' Groats

ALPS CROSS—BORDER ROUTES

100 Hut Walks in the Alps
Alpine Ski Mountaineering Vol 1 — Western Alps
The Karnischer Hohenweg
The Tour of the Bernina
Trail Running — Chamonix and the Mont Blanc region
Trekking Chamonix to Zermatt
Trekking in the Alps
Trekking in the Silvretta and Ratikon Alps
Trekking Munich to Venice
Trekking the Tour du Mont Blanc
Tour du Mont Blanc Map Booklet
Walking in the Alps

FRANCE, BELGIUM, AND LUXEMBOURG

Camino de Santiago — Via Podiensis
Chamonix Mountain Adventures
Cycle Touring in France
Cycling London to Paris
Cycling the Canal de la Garonne
Cycling the Canal du Midi
Mont Blanc Walks
Mountain Adventures in the Maurienne
Short Treks on Corsica
The GR5 Trail
The GR5 Trail — Vosges and Jura
Benelux and Lorraine
The Grand Traverse of the Massif Central
The Moselle Cycle Route
Trekking in the Vanoise

Trekking the Cathar Way
Trekking the GR10
Trekking the GR20 Corsica
Trekking the Robert Louis Stevenson Trail
Via Ferratas of the French Alps
Walking in Provence — East
Walking in Provence — West
Walking in the Auvergne
Walking in the Briançonnais
Walking in the Dordogne
Walking in the Haute Savoie: North
Walking in the Haute Savoie: South
Walking on Corsica
Walking the Brittany Coast Path
Walking in the Ardennes

PYRENEES AND FRANCE/SPAIN CROSS—BORDER ROUTES

Shorter Treks in the Pyrenees
The Pyrenean Haute Route
The Pyrenees
Trekking the Cami dels Bons Homes
Trekking the GR11 Trail
Walks and Climbs in the Pyrenees

SPAIN AND PORTUGAL

Camino de Santiago: Camino Frances
Costa Blanca Mountain Adventures
Cycling the Camino de Santiago
Mountain Walking in Mallorca
Mountain Walking in Southern Catalunya
Spain's Sendero Historico: The GR1
The Andalucian Coast to Coast Walk
The Camino del Norte and Camino Primitivo
The Camino Ingles and Ruta do Mar
The Mountains Around Nerja
The Sierras of Extremadura
Trekking in Mallorca
Trekking in the Canary Islands
Trekking the GR7 in Andalucia
Walking and Trekking in the Sierra Nevada
Walking in Andalucia
Walking in Catalunya — Barcelona
Girona Pyrenees
Walking in the Picos de Europa
Walking La Via de la Plata and Camino Sanabres
Walking on Gran Canaria
Walking on La Gomera and El Hierro
Walking on La Palma
Walking on Lanzarote and Fuerteventura
Walking on Tenerife
Walking on the Costa Blanca
Walking the Camino dos Faros
Portugal's Rota Vicentina
The Camino Portugues
Walking in Portugal
Walking in the Algarve

Walking on Madeira
Walking on the Azores

SWITZERLAND
Switzerland's Jura Crest Trail
The Swiss Alps
Tour of the Jungfrau Region
Trekking the Swiss Via Alpina
Walking in Arolla and Zinal
Walking in the Bernese Oberland
— Jungfrau region
Walking in the Engadine —
Switzerland
Walking in the Valais
Walking in Ticino
Walking in Zermatt and Saas—Fee

GERMANY
Hiking and Cycling in the
Black Forest
The Danube Cycleway Vol 1
The Rhine Cycle Route
The Westweg
Walking in the Bavarian Alps

POLAND, SLOVAKIA, ROMANIA, HUNGARY AND BULGARIA
The Danube Cycleway Vol 2
The High Tatras
The Mountains of Romania

SCANDINAVIA, ICELAND AND GREENLAND
Hiking in Norway — South
Trekking the Kungsleden
Trekking in Greenland — The
Arctic Circle Trail
Walking and Trekking in Iceland

SLOVENIA, CROATIA, SERBIA, MONTENEGRO AND ALBANIA
Hiking Slovenia's Juliana Trail
Mountain Biking in Slovenia
The Islands of Croatia
The Julian Alps of Slovenia
The Mountains of Montenegro
The Peaks of the Balkans Trail
The Slovene Mountain Trail
Walking in Slovenia:
The Karavanke
Walks and Treks in Croatia

ITALY
Alta Via 1 — Trekking in the
Dolomites
Alta Via 2 — Trekking in the
Dolomites
Day Walks in the Dolomites
Italy's Grande Traversata delle Alpi
Italy's Sibillini National Park
Ski Touring and Snowshoeing in
the Dolomites
The Way of St Francis
Trekking Gran Paradiso: Alta Via 2
Trekking in the Apennines

Trekking the Giants' Trail:
Alta Via 1 through the Italian
Pennine Alps
Via Ferratas of the Italian Dolomites
Vol 1
Vol 2
Walking in Abruzzo
Walking in Italy's Cinque Terre
Walking in Italy's Stelvio National
Park
Walking in Sicily
Walking in the Aosta Valley
Walking in the Dolomites
Walking in Tuscany
Walking in Umbria
Walking Lake Como and Maggiore
Walking Lake Garda and Iseo
Walking on the Amalfi Coast
Walks and Treks in the Maritime Alps

IRELAND
The Wild Atlantic Way and
Western Ireland
Walking the Kerry Way
Walking the Wicklow Way

EUROPEAN CYCLING
Cycling the Route des Grandes Alpes
Cycling the Ruta Via de la Plata
The Elbe Cycle Route
The River Loire Cycle Route
The River Rhone Cycle Route

INTERNATIONAL CHALLENGES, COLLECTIONS AND ACTIVITIES
Europe's High Points
Walking the Via Francigena
Pilgrim Route —
Part 1
Part 2
Part 3

AUSTRIA
Innsbruck Mountain Adventures
Trekking Austria's Adlerweg
Trekking in Austria's Hohe Tauern
Trekking in Austria's Zillertal Alps
Trekking in the Stubai Alps
Walking in Austria
Walking in the Salzkammergut:
the Austrian Lake District

MEDITERRANEAN
The High Mountains of Crete
Trekking in Greece
Walking and Trekking in Zagori
Walking and Trekking on Corfu
Walking on the Greek Islands —
the Cyclades
Walking in Cyprus
Walking on Malta

HIMALAYA
8000 metres
Everest: A Trekker's Guide
Trekking in the Karakoram

NORTH AMERICA
Hiking and Cycling the California
Missions Trail
The John Muir Trail
The Pacific Crest Trail

SOUTH AMERICA
Aconcagua and the Southern Andes
Hiking and Biking Peru's Inca Trails
Trekking in Torres del Paine

AFRICA
Kilimanjaro
Walking in the Drakensberg
Walks and Scrambles in the
Moroccan Anti-Atlas

NEW ZEALAND AND AUSTRALIA
Hiking the Overland Track

CHINA, JAPAN, AND ASIA
Annapurna
Hiking and Trekking in the Japan
Alps and Mount Fuji
Hiking in Hong Kong
Japan's Kumano Kodo Pilgrimage
Trekking in Bhutan
Trekking in Ladakh
Trekking in Tajikistan
Trekking in the Himalaya

TECHNIQUES
Fastpacking
The Mountain Hut Book

MINI GUIDES
Alpine Flowers
Navigation
Pocket First Aid and
Wilderness Medicine
Snow

MOUNTAIN LITERATURE
A Walk in the Clouds
Abode of the Gods
Fifty Years of Adventure
The Pennine Way —
the Path, the People, the Journey
Unjustifiable Risk?

For full information on all our
guides, books and eBooks,
visit our website:
www.cicerone.co.uk

CICERONE

Trust Cicerone to guide your next adventure,
wherever it may be around the world...

Discover guides for hiking, mountain walking, backpacking,
trekking, trail running, cycling and mountain biking, ski touring,
climbing and scrambling in Britain, Europe and worldwide.

Connect with Cicerone online and find inspiration.

- buy books and ebooks
- articles, advice and trip reports
- podcasts and live events
- GPX files and updates
- regular newsletter

cicerone.co.uk